The Lost Art of Sacrifice

Also by Vicki Burbach
from Sophia Institute Press

How to Read Your Way to Heaven
A Spiritual Reading Program for the Worst of Sinners,
the Greatest of Saints, and Everyone in Between

Vicki Burbach

The LOST ART
of
SACRIFICE

A Spiritual Guide for
Denying Yourself,
Embracing the Cross,
and Finding Joy

SOPHIA INSTITUTE PRESS
Manchester, New Hampshire

Sophia Institute Press
Box 5284, Manchester, NH 03108
1-800-888-9344

www.SophiaInstitute.com

Sophia Institute Press® is a registered trademark of Sophia Institute.

paperback ISBN 978-1-622826-360

ebook ISBN 978-1-622826-377

Library of Congress Control Number: 2020952740

First printing

To the Sacred Heart of Jesus
and for Dale,
who embodies sacrificial love
on a daily basis

The modern world, which denies personal guilt
and admits only social crimes,
which has no place for personal repentance
but only public reforms,
has divorced Christ from His Cross;
the Bridegroom and the Bride
have been pulled apart.
What God hath joined together,
men have torn asunder.

—Archbishop Fulton Sheen, *Life of Christ*

Contents

Acknowledgments xi

Foreword xiii

Introduction 1

Part 1
The Fundamentals of Sacrifice

1. What Is Sacrifice? 9

2. Surrender Yourself to Freedom 17

3. Lose the "Me" Attitudes 23

4. Contemplate the Cross. 35

5. Become One with Christ. 45

Part 2
Avoiding Satan's Traps

6. Beware the Traps of Modernism:
Lies about Spiritual Traditions 59

7. Beware of Blessings and Curses:
The Lie of the Prosperity Gospel. 73

8. Beware of Wolves in Sheep's Clothing:
   The Lie of Socialism 89

9. Beware the Gospel of Death:
   Lies about Suffering 99

10. Beware the Temptation to Throw in the Towel:
    Lies about Willpower 115

Part 3

The Art of Sacrifice

11. Dispositions That Make Way for Sacrifice. 133

12. Penance and Mortification. 151

13. Love of God: Giving God Your Time 159

14. Love of God: Devotion to Christ and His Mother 175

15. Love of Neighbor. 189

16. Perseverance and the Road to Holiness 203

    Conclusion: Final Prayer for You. 213

    Appendix: The Discipline of Holy Mother Church . . . 215

    About the Author 223

Acknowledgments

This project was, in itself, a lesson in sacrifice. I am thankful to John Barger, founder of Sophia Institute Press, for his honest feedback a year ago when he told me that readers would be better served if we delayed publication so that I could cut my behemoth of a manuscript in half. Thank you also to editors Anna Maria Mendell and Nora Malone, who have worked tirelessly to help me tweak the final product in record time; it was a pleasure to work with both of you!

Over the past two years, countless friends and acquaintances have read parts of this book and offered feedback. I cannot possibly name all of you, but you know who you are! I would like to offer a special thank you to Regina Heywood, who graciously made herself available whenever I needed something read and reviewed in a pinch! Thanks also to my mother, Donna Wilson, and sister, Tanya Koller, who allowed me to work in a spare room whenever I needed a quiet space.

Thank you to my husband, Dale, and to our children, Christian, Caleb, Emma, Noelle, Elias, and Marlena, for supporting me and for allowing me the time for research and writing ... and cutting and rewriting. This project has taken much longer than you bargained for. I pray that through all of your sacrifices over these two years, the joy of sacrifice may spread far and wide.

More than anything, I am thankful to Christ, my Savior, who knows more than anyone my penchant for self-gratification and self-indulgence, and yet (perhaps because of these weaknesses), He still calls me to appreciate and to share the art of sacrifice.

Foreword

In developed countries, the flesh rules and all is oriented to this reign of self-destruction. Whatever taste, temperature, time, or other specific desire we have, we can find it—quickly and in abundance—legal or illegal. On the more positive side, this can appear to be a blessing. For example, what can be wrong with fast access to food we like? But instead of making our lives better, this indulgence actually reverses the intended role of our lower and higher natures.

Because of concupiscence, our lower nature, our cravings for things of the flesh always seek to rule us. The powerful reign of our appetites and desires relentlessly drives us to the seven deadly sins and their offspring—all of which, unchecked, will lead us to Hell. At best, these desires enslave us to the wants and whims of our feelings rather than our intellect and will. This enslavement, as St. John of the Cross reveals, leads to a darkened, defiled, and weakened will. This is the pathway into habitual mortal sin, total internal disintegration, anxiety, stress, and ultimate separation from God.

The solution is found in one simple command of Jesus, "Take up your cross and follow me," and in the Holy Spirit's commensurate admonition through St. Paul: "I punish my body and enslave it" (1 Cor. 9:27, NRSV). When we read these admonitions, we might have some inkling of what they mean, but living them out is far more difficult than talking about them. This is where Vicki Burbach's work is so important for us and for the Church. She provides a pathway to reinvigorating the lost art of ascesis — of saying yes to God and no to the flesh —; yes to our higher calling and purpose and no to the pull of dissolution. This process of reordering the flesh so that it is subordinate to the spirit is essential to knowing the peace of God and to the soul's progress toward sanctity.

—Dan Burke

Introduction

Truly, truly I say to you, unless a grain of wheat
falls into the earth and dies, it remains alone;
but if it dies, it bears much fruit.

—John 12:24

We are living in trying times. The world seems to have lost its way, and so many of us feel powerless to correct its course. We begin each day wondering what happened to the world we once knew, and some are fearful of the future. But it's very possible that Our Lord has allowed this opportunity in history as a reminder for us that this world is passing away (1 John 2:17). Perhaps now is a perfect time to step back from material things and remember that there is something more for which we were made. As Christians, our allegiance is not to this world, but to God alone, through His Son, our Lord and Savior, Jesus Christ. So what should we do? Perhaps we should take this time to return to our roots, examining what it means to be a Christian in the world today.

What does it mean to be a Christian? What does it mean to follow Christ? Two thousand years ago, it meant a complete transformation of one's heart, mind, and soul. It often meant a willingness to endure torture and death. It meant knowing the promise of an eternal life that was infinitely more valuable than the world in which we live. That promise provided Christians with a purpose that transcended the pleasures of this life. For early Christians, the Cross was part of their identity, and they didn't shy away from it. Rather, they passionately pursued their mission, whatever the cost.

What was that mission? It was to bring the Gospel to every man, woman and child, opening hearts to God's grace, that He might draw every soul to Himself. Christians recognized that this mission required a life of sacrifice; a denial of "self." It meant cooperating with the Master Gardener as He pruned and formed them, ridding their hearts and souls of all that might obscure Him from view. For they knew that in order to accomplish their mission, they must be able to say with St. Paul, "I have been crucified with Christ; it is no longer I who live, but Christ who lives in me" (Gal. 2:20).

Today, this mission remains the same. Sadly, there is little evidence in the world of the Christianity of old. Our secular culture celebrates the temporal over the spiritual, and many of us have been seduced by the daily demands and attractions of the here and now. As a result, many have drifted from the passionate Christianity of earlier times. In fact, in recent generations, Christianity has even developed a reputation in the West for soft sentimentalism. Christ has been reduced to tender emotion and unconditional love, wrapped up in a nonjudgmental blanket of relativism. This is what Archbishop Fulton Sheen referred to as Christ without His Cross.[1] Many Christians no longer strive to engage in lives of prayer and sacrifice in order to carry out

---

[1] Fulton J. Sheen, *Life of Christ* (New York: Image Books, 2008), xxiv–xxv.

the Great Commission—and most aren't even aware of what has been lost. Rather than seeking to reunite Christ with His Cross, they have destroyed the Cross altogether and used the scraps to build a sort of progressive humanitarian religion based on materialism and self-entitlement.

This development should cause grave concern for those of us who truly desire to follow Christ, for how can one follow in His footsteps if the Way has been obscured by generations of distortions and misrepresentations?

It seems the only solution to this problem is to return to Christ's words and find out what He actually said to His would-be followers. We owe it to ourselves and to Him to consider His call as He made it, unblemished by the mores of the culture:

> If any man would come after me, let him deny himself and take up his cross and follow me. For whoever would save his life will lose it, and whoever loses his life for my sake will find it. For what will it profit a man, if he gains the whole world and forfeits his life? (Matt. 16:24–26)

The question is, how do we go about doing this? What does denying myself look like? How exactly must I carry my cross?

Not only are we to deny ourselves and take up our crosses, but we are to follow Christ in the process. And although we might be tempted to assume we are following Him through the pearly gates to an eternal Paradise with the Father, many of us have somehow been indoctrinated to overlook a major stop along the way.

Before He leads us to Paradise, Christ leads us to Calvary.

Like Christ, we are called to carry the cross and to be crucified. Of course, we can ask the Simons in our lives to help us make our way along the path, and we may certainly help them as well. But at the end of our fated journey, whether that journey is a moment of consideration for someone else or a lifetime of pain and suffering, each of us will be asked to climb right up there alongside Christ and sacrifice our very lives. By this I don't necessarily mean that we are called to be martyrs, offering our blood as a testament of our allegiance to Christ—although, for some of us, that call may come—but rather that we offer ourselves as "bloodless" martyrs, ready to release our attachments, our desires, our preferences, our idiosyncrasies, our very wills, in deference to the will of God. Essentially, we are called to die to ourselves.

And if we don't? Say we decide to climb down from the hill of Calvary and save our lives—that is, hold on to our attachments; prioritize our wants, desires, and preferences; and put ourselves first? Well, according to Christ, in saving my own life, I will surely lose it. *But*—and here's the clincher—if I climb up on that cross, enduring to the end, all in effort to lose my life for Christ's sake; if I unite my will to the will of God, denying myself by offering myself; in that case, I am bound to find my life—and no doubt I will have it abundantly (John 10:10).

There is no greater paradox in all the world than the paradox of the Cross.

Yes, sacrifice is hard.

But our souls were made for sacrifice. And deep down in the farthest corners of our hearts, in places that we keep hidden even from ourselves, we know that this is true.

Sadly, generations of comfort and excess and expectations have weakened our wills. In fact, there are many who argue for the need to scrap the concept of willpower altogether. We have grown soft. We have lost our way in a world of materialism and self-determination. We have slipped from the cross, even denying Christ, in order to avoid that call that speaks directly to the depths of our hearts.

Introduction

So how can we find our way back to the cross? How can we reconnect to the root of our very souls? How can we find that part of us that absolutely knows we were made for love? For sacrifice? We may be moved by the contributions made to the world by our fellow man, and inspired by all the saints who've gone before us; but how can we bring ourselves to *participate* in the type of life for which we were made? How can we find the joy that is waiting for us?

Whatever your experience with the cross, whether you struggle with a painful and debilitating illness or with finding joy in the little interruptions in life, it is my prayer that through these pages you might reclaim the lost art of sacrifice.

Part 1

The Fundamentals of Sacrifice

Come to him, to that living stone, rejected by men
but in God's sight chosen and precious;
and like living stones be yourselves built
into a spiritual house, to be a holy priesthood,
to offer spiritual sacrifices acceptable to God
through Jesus Christ.

—1 Peter 2:4–5

On the wall of my office hangs a beautiful picture of St. Teresa of Calcutta with the following quotation from her as a constant reminder:

A sacrifice to be real must cost, must hurt, and must empty ourselves.

There are many levels of "cost" associated with the gifts of sacrifice we offer. Sometimes in the midst of the struggle, alone like one simple tree in a glorious wood, it can be a challenge to see the awe-inspiring montage as a great and magnificent forest; or to know that within that colossal forest, each and every effort, however fragile, is contained and blessed and serves to fill out a breathtaking whole. It is the abundant foliage that lives and breathes and gives life. God will do amazing things with the smallest of gifts.

The quotation from Mother Teresa continues:

> Give yourself fully to God. He will use you to accomplish great things on the condition that you believe much more in His love than in your weakness.

This is the nature of sacrifice, the free gift of yourself. The what, when, where, why, and how of sacrifice is the subject of this book. But before we get too far into the whys and wherefores, perhaps we should begin with the what. In part 1, we'll discuss the true meaning of sacrifice and its place in our daily lives.

1

What Is Sacrifice?

God, give me a hard life but let it be beautiful, rich and aspiring.

—Janusz Korczak, prayer from his youth, *Ghetto Diary*

The name Janusz Korczak might not ring a bell for many Americans, but in Europe, he is as well known as Ann Frank.[2] Korczak was a pen name for Dr. Henryk Goldszmit, a pediatrician who achieved relative fame in Poland as the author of several popular books both for and about children.[3] His love for children resulted in Korczak's founding a Jewish orphanage in Warsaw in 1912. His dedication to the children in his care would direct the course of the rest of his life.

Shortly after Germany invaded Warsaw in 1939, Korczak's orphans were forcibly transferred to the Warsaw Ghetto, a rundown prison of a place with walls that soared over ten feet high, topped with barbed wire and flanked by few points of entry, which were heavily guarded to prevent escape. More than

---

[2] Betty Jean Lifton, *The King of Children: A Biography of Janusz Korczak* (New York: Farrar, Straus & Giroux, 1988), 17.

[3] Biography of Janusz Korczak, Janusz Korczak Association of Canada, http://www.januszkorczak.ca/biography.html.

450,000 Jews were housed in the ghetto, which spanned only 1.3 square miles of land.[4] By virtue of his esteemed reputation in Poland, Korczak was offered refuge on the outside; but he declined, opting to relocate with his orphans and to continue as their caretaker.

Those banished to the ghetto were undernourished and over-crowded. Typhus was rampant as quarters were full of rats and lice. Occupants spent winters without heat and without enough clothes, and hundreds succumbed to the elements. Korczak spent much time begging for food in order to keep his children from starving. His body deteriorated, but he continued to persevere despite the horrific conditions they were forced to endure.[5]

In 1942, rumors began that trains were coming to retrieve members of the ghetto in order to take them to Treblinka, a sparse camp in the northeast corner of Warsaw that housed nothing but a small factory and six gas chambers. In August, just before the trains arrived, Korczak was again offered refuge, that he might not board the train. Again he declined. Instead, witnesses watched from second-story windows and rooftops as Janusz Korczak, along with 196 children, stepped calmly out of the orphanage. Not one of them tried to escape; rather, they all walked obediently with Korczak to meet the train, which consisted of a series of red cattle cars. Victims were packed in like animals.

A *third time*, Korczak was offered a way out. It is said that an SS officer, who recognized him as the author of one of his favorite children's books, offered to help him escape. Korczak kindly

---

[4] "Warsaw Ghetto," Yad Vashem, http://www.yadvashem.org/holocaust/about/ghettos/warsaw.html.

[5] Janusz Korczak, *Ghetto Diary* (New Haven, CT: Yale University Press, 2003), https://archive.org/stream/GhettoDiary-English-JanuszKorczak/ghettodiary_djvu.txt.

thanked the man before boarding the train with his children. Once on board, the sliding doors were slammed together and locked. Korczak and his children were never heard from again.

Mary Berg describes the scene in her *Diary from the Warsaw Ghetto*:

> The orphanage of Doctor Janusz Korczak is now empty. A few days ago we all stood by the window and watched the Germans surround the buildings. Ranks of children holding hands began to come out of the gate. Among them were the little ones, two, three years old. The oldest may have been thirteen. Each child held a bundle in his hand. All wore white aprons. They walked in pairs calmly and even with a smile. They had no premonition of their destiny. At the end of this march walked Korczak who was guarding the children that they wouldn't diverge. From time to time, with his fatherly care, he tapped on a child's head or arm and straightened the ranks. He was wearing high boots with trouser legs inside them, alpaca jacket and a navy blue cap, the so-called Maciejowka cap. He walked confidently in the company of a doctor from the orphanage dressed in a white apron. The sad march disappeared around the corner of Dzielna and Smocza Streets.... The house is now empty, except for the gendarmes who are still emptying out the bedrooms of the murdered children.[6]

Rather than accept offers of asylum, Korczak chose to stand with the insignificant, the unwanted, the orphan. Rather than allow these orphans to face suffering or death alone, this man

---

[6] Mary Berg, *The Diary of Mary Berg: Growing up in the Warsaw Ghetto* (London: Oneworld, 2013), 136.

opted to hold their hands. Janusz Korczak offered his very life as a *sacrifice*.

WHEN THE ORDINARY BECOMES
EXTRAORDINARY

Sacrifice at its core consists in understanding the relationship between God and man, between Creator and creature, between Father and child. This understanding of who God is and who we are in relation to Him is critical to both the ability and the desire to sacrifice. For sacrifice requires the subjugation of oneself to the omnipotent God, the offering of oneself as a gift, ultimately in service to God.

In his book *Introduction to Christianity*, Joseph Ratzinger asserts that the beginning of our Credo unites Christians with their Jewish brothers and sisters:

> I believe in God, the Father, the almighty, the Creator. This statement, with which Christians have been professing their faith in God for almost two thousand years, is the product of a still older history. Behind it stands Israel's daily profession of faith, the Christian form of which it represents: "Hear, O Israel, Yahweh, thy God, is an only God." With its first words the Christian creed takes up the creed of Israel and takes up with it Israel's striving, its experience of faith, and its struggle for God.[7]

In the Judeo-Christian tradition, we affirm that there is one God, and in choosing Him, we denounce not only Satan and

---

[7] Joseph Cardinal Ratzinger, Introduction to Christianity (Ignatius Press: San Francisco, 2004), 110.

his evil works but all other gods as well. Ratzinger refers to the three main forms of polytheism as the "worship of bread, the worship of love, and the idolization of power." In choosing God, we renounce all the rest.

In choosing to offer not only his last breath, but the many years of his life, to care for the poor, the orphan, and the helpless, Korczak rejected all other gods. He prayed as a boy, "God, give me a hard life but let it be beautiful, rich and aspiring."[8] True to his Jewish heritage, he devoted himself to the recognition of the one and only *Yahweh*, the great I AM. In his devotion, Korczak offered himself for something greater than himself, implicitly understanding that recognition of God as absolute is what gives life meaning.

The word *sacrifice* comes from the Latin roots *sacer*, "sacred," and *facere*, "to do or perform."[9] Even outside the Judeo-Christian tradition, whatever the religion, sacrifice has always had something to do with the divine or the sacred. Our ancestors made burnt offerings to God, calling them sacrifices. Over time, the word *sacrifice* has developed other connotations, as in the sense of "something given up for the sake of another"[10] (not necessarily for God) or of giving up something to make our lives better, such as sacrificing for a better lifestyle or engaging in a fitness program. But traditionally, sacrifice has meant *the offering of something for a sacred purpose*. Anything *sacred* is *extraordinary*. It is not of this world. It is of God. And its goodness extends far beyond our experience. Today, our sacrifices look very different from those of

---

[8] Korczak, *Ghetto Diary*, 64.
[9] *Online Etymology Dictionary*, s.v. "sacrifice," https://www.etym online.com/word/sacrifice.
[10] Ibid.

our Old Testament brothers and sisters, but they are nonetheless offered as an act of worship for love of God.

Despite the darkness that descended upon the world through the unleashing and spreading of horrific evil, Janusz Korczak provided the light, an *extraordinary* light through which the world could continue to move forward. Through his strength and compassion, he offered the Face of God—which is Christ—to the world. His sacrifice provided hope and therefore purpose for those who remained. In addition to Korczak's, there were many other sacrifices made in the face of the evils of the Holocaust. Every single one provides hope and inspiration for each of us, serving as a healing salve for the gaping wound that unspeakable evil inflicted upon the Body of Christ.

Certainly our sacrifices, performed as sacred gifts to a loving God are extraordinary. When we examine the effects of sacrifice—whether our own or those around us—we can see that sacrifices offered in love move us beyond the self, pulling us out of our comfort zones and helping to unite us to our fellow man. Serving God through serving others makes us better than we are, and yet sometimes it's easy to forget that our sacrifices also make us more notably *human*. In performing a sacrifice—a pure act of love for God—we emulate *Christ, the perfect human being*, whose entire earthly life consisted of sacrifice, culminating in His death on the Cross for our salvation.

CULTIVATING THE ART OF SACRIFICE

When we begin a journey, we need to know where we're going. In this case, our destination is perfect union with God. Equally important when we begin a journey is to know our starting point. Where are we on the map, and in which direction should we go to reach our destination?

Action

Complete an examination of your relationship to sacrifice:

1. Think about the definition of sacrifice offered in this chapter. Now ask yourself where sacrifice comes most easily to you. Do you find it easiest to serve your community, your spouse, your children, or God? Why does sacrifice comes most easily to you in that area? Think about your motivation. Is it love, or is it that you seek approval and are worried about what people think of you? Perhaps you sacrifice out of obligation or for other motivations. Name your *why* and keep it in mind.

2. Where do you struggle most to offer sacrifices? In what area of your life is God calling you to give more? Your marriage? Family? Friends? Work? There may be several areas. Note each one. But highlight that area that causes the greatest challenge for you at this time. Why is sacrifice a challenge in this area? Is it because of selfishness, lack of time, or another factor? Name your *why* here as well and keep it in mind as you read.

Suggested Reading

You Shall Worship One God, by Fr. Marie-Dominique Philippe
Introduction to Christianity, by Joseph Cardinal Ratzinger

2

Surrender Yourself to Freedom

*Learn to follow the movements of grace, and
thou wilt know how easy is the law of Christ;
for it will carry thee rather than thou it.*

—St. Claude de la Colombière[11]

When I was in college, I taught swimming lessons for the Boys
and Girls Clubs of America. Every session with new swimmers
would begin the same way. After a hesitant slip into the pool,
my beginner students would hold on to the edge with white-
knuckled little hands, shivering and scared, but with wide, wary
eyes they signaled a great desire to break free of the wall. They
wanted so desperately to glide across that pool with their arms
outstretched and their legs strong and free. Only one thing held
them back: fear.

One at a time, I would coax those little ones out into the
water with me, and they would wrap their arms around my neck
and cling for dear life. It never failed that the most challenging
skill to teach them was to float on their backs. I'd hold out my

---

[11] Claude de la Colombière, *The Spiritual Retreat* (London: James
Duffy, Wellington-Quay and Paternoster Row, 1863), 81.

hand and gently encourage a student to turn over, tilting his head back against the surface of the water, with his legs outstretched, but relaxed, and I would support him gently beneath the small of his back, coaxing him to surrender his fears and his need to be in control, that he might relax upon the surface of the water.

To say that effort was an exercise in patience would be an understatement. But finally, there came a moment, a turning point, if you will. From that point, a student could make considerable progress. That moment came precisely when my student realized that he could get along much better in the water by surrendering his control, by allowing his body to rest comfortably amid the gentle sway of the water, trusting that my hand would stay securely beneath him as long as necessary, until he could begin to work with me toward all the other skills he sought to acquire.

One day when I was frustrated by my inability to make progress in the spiritual life, I realized that those of us who struggle are like those new swimmers I worked with so long ago. This is especially true when we think our environment is out of our control. Rather than trust in God, we believe that in order to find security, we must maintain exacting control over everything in our personal lives. We strain to stretch our legs in precise angles, contorting our arms just so, and we lift our heads to see whether we are doing things correctly. And what happens when a swimmer lifts his head while trying to float? He sinks. That's what we do. We sink. We try so hard to control every movement, to be exacting and precise. And we forget that we would find everything we are searching for if only we would surrender our control to our Heavenly Father.

It is a mistake to believe that salvation is dependent on human endeavors and that if only we can be determined enough, disciplined enough, focused enough, holy enough, we can, in effect, earn our way to Heaven or buy God's favor by our efforts. Those who believe this are nonswimmers who spend anxious and frustrated lives condemned to the side of the pool, never knowing the peace, joy, and freedom that come with trust and surrender.

We are not to place our faith in our human nature and our capacity to control our environment, our desires, our actions, or our thoughts; rather, we are to cooperate with God's grace. It is not about our power to save ourselves, but about His power to save us.

SACRIFICE AND SURRENDER

Surrender is the abandonment of our wills to God's will. It is allowing ourselves to be vulnerable — to trust in His providence. Surrender is about accepting what comes rather than perfectly juggling those balls that are your spiritual, physical, familial, and community obligations. Surrender is trusting God with all the balls, rather than trying to juggle them all by yourself.

So sacrifice, while it may seem from afar to be all about tying your hands and binding your feet, forbidding all freedom and enslaving yourself (in a bad way), in fact, your body and soul will be most free and most happy when you surrender yourself completely to God. Let Him direct your path. Let go of your misguided notions about your control, as these are based in pride, which will not only cause you to fail but will undermine the very gifts you wish to give. God is our beginning and our end; He created us and also, by His grace, will welcome us into His house for all eternity.

But letting go can be hard. Particularly in our fast-paced, hyperscheduled, jam-packed culture. The fact is that surrender is a concept diametrically opposed to the American spirit.

After all, we are a nation founded on phrases such as Patrick Henry's famous "Give me liberty or give me death." Echoing heroically in the recesses of our minds are the words of Winston Churchill—that half-American Brit with a deeply American stubborn streak—"We shall never surrender!"

So how do we go about achieving the discipline that allows us to align our wills with the will of God while surrendering our own desires, plans, dreams—in fact, our very lives—to God? That's a tall order. Surrender doesn't come cheap—particularly in certain areas of life.

What must we do? We must be open to God's grace in our lives. We must be open to the movement of the Holy Spirit. We must prepare ourselves to be ready when the opportunity to cooperate comes along.

But how do we prepare ourselves?[12]

LOVE: THE GREAT MOTIVATOR

Sacrifice is easiest and most efficacious and most *authentic* when it is a pure gift of love. When we offer gifts for love of Christ alone, whether forgoing a sin that seems to hold our affections or giving up a material good that we enjoy, our sacrifices are best made out of love for God and complete trust in Him.

According to St. Claude de la Colombière, "They that deliver themselves up liberally to God shall renew their strength, they shall take wings, as eagles, they shall fly and not be weary."[13]

Love makes sacrifice easier. If you have children, just think about how much you would be willing to sacrifice for them. How

[12] De la Colombière, *The Spiritual Retreat*, 82.
[13] Ibid., 83.

much do you sacrifice for them already? How often do you cook, clean, comfort, discipline, work, and suffer for your kids without even giving it a second thought? That's what love does. It causes us to sacrifice as a gift—without even thinking twice about it. We must cultivate love in our hearts in order to be able to surrender all to God.

When everything we do is done with the sole purpose of pleasing God out of love, sacrifice becomes not a chore, not a discipline, but a gift that is just an outgrowth of love. And remember, anything done out of love, no matter how small, is of inestimable value in the eyes of God.

There is no freedom like the freedom of a man who has released the weight of the world from his shoulders. And that is the freedom that comes with surrender. To surrender means to trust God. And in that trust, we need no longer live in fear. Trust breeds inner peace, no matter the chaos or tragedy that might threaten us. Instead of stressing over things beyond our control, we can offer them to God. Just like the swimmer flailing away at summer camp, handing over that control is the first and most important step toward growth. Ultimately, surrender will allow us to grow in holiness. We will no longer need to struggle but will be able to make wonderful sacrifices grounded in love alone. Rather than stress about things that are beyond our control, we can choose to trust God, and we will be free to love—free to sacrifice. "Now the Lord is the Spirit, and where the Spirit of the Lord is, there is freedom" (2 Cor. 3:17).

CULTIVATING THE ART OF SACRIFICE

God is holding His hands out to You. He would like nothing more than for you to turn to Him for every need and to seek His help at all times. He desires that you live without anxiety, that, in trust, you unite your will to His, that you might learn to live a life of sacrificial love. Are you ready to surrender? If not, spend some time in prayer, asking the Holy Spirit to reveal what is keeping you from complete surrender. What are you holding on to that prevents you from giving yourself completely?

Action

Ask God what He would like you to sacrifice right now. It may be something as simple as setting time aside to spend with Him. It may be as challenging as giving up a strong attachment that you've been clinging to. Whatever it is, ask Him to help you make that offering in love. If you can't quite bring yourself to make the sacrifice, keep trying. And keep asking.

Suggested Reading

Trustful Surrender to Divine Providence, by St. Claude de la Colombière
Spiritual Combat, by Lorenzo Scupoli

3

Lose the "Me" Attitudes

This, in fact, is my task: to do my different duties without anyone's suspecting what trouble I have in reconciling them, to forget myself, to develop what God has given me of reason and intelligence, to banish pride even in the most subtle forms I know so well, to love strongly without self-seeking, to accept by divine grace the duty of every day and hour and never to neglect it, however small it may be. I shall often fall, but that help from above for which I shall humbly petition daily will not fail me. Besides, to live is to fight, to suffer, and to love.

—Servant of God Elisabeth Leseur[14]

Mr. Holland's Opus, starring Richard Dreyfuss, follows the fictional life of talented musician and composer Glenn Holland from his early days of married life, when he works nights for a band while spending the day at his piano, sans income, composing what he hopes someday will become his masterpiece. Immediately into the film, Holland takes on a stable position as a high school

---

[14] *The Secret Diary of Elisabeth Leseur: The Woman Whose Goodness Changed Her Husband from Atheist to Priest* (Manchester, NH: Sophia Institute Press, 2002), 26.

music teacher to support his family. From the very first moment, it is clear that Holland is *not* in love with his job.

As the movie progresses, we witness firsthand Holland's frustrations with all of life's curves. His days are full of work, and his nights are full of family obligations, all of which he sees as burdensome because they serve to keep him from achieving his dream. Over time, and almost against his will, Holland develops a love for his students as he introduces innovative methods of teaching to inspire their passion for music. We watch as year after year passes and class after class graduates. Sadly, but for a spark here or a nugget there, Holland feels most of his time has been all but wasted. His opus — of course — is never completed, never sold.

Eventually, after thirty years, Holland retires as an older man, past his prime. But — bring tissues for the climax — as he walks into a giant surprise assembly in the auditorium, he quickly realizes (as does the viewer) that all his time was not wasted at all. Through the years, Holland has served countless people, most of whom have achieved things they never thought possible. Dozens of grateful students representing various classes that have graduated through the years come to pay tribute to Holland's inspiration and devotion. The viewer comes away feeling that Holland's life had meaning beyond his dreams. Every person he served — family, students, even teachers whom he befriended — were better for their relationships with Glenn Holland. All those people? *They* were his opus; his life's work; his greatest achievement.

When I first watched this movie, I was aghast at the thought of not achieving my life's ambition. Back then, my material dreams were young and fresh, and the landscape before me was vast and flowing with possibility. The idea of not achieving my dreams was unthinkable. I thought, why couldn't Holland have done both? Why did he have to be just a teacher? Why couldn't he accomplish his dream and affect others through his music? The entire plot of Mr. *Holland's Opus* seemed like a cop-out to me. It was a movie for all those who failed to achieve their lifelong dreams and needed a consolation prize. I was much more into inspirational films that showed the grit and grime of making things happen—of accomplishing dreams against all odds, no matter the obstacle, no matter the sacrifice.

Twenty years later, I get it. Life happens. Dreams have a way of stepping into the shadows, quietly waiting while we deal with the more immediate demands on our time. So often, the unexpected steps in to upend our plans. We suffer personal tragedy, job losses, illness, the consequences of foolish decisions, and so much more.

What do we do about that? Some choose to abandon other obligations to pursue their own "happiness" at any cost, telling themselves that life is short and regrets are ruthless. Many in our culture applaud that choice. We are all told, after all, that life is all about self-fulfillment and personal happiness.

You may want to think before you jump ship. People who chase their happiness at the expense of their relationships and responsibilities often encounter yet another paradox of wisdom. The more you focus on material happiness, the less happy you will be. In our desperate attempts to save ourselves, to fulfill our desires, and to achieve our goals, we often come up empty-handed in the end. On the other hand, when we let go of our own desires, our pleasure, and our fulfillment, we allow ourselves to achieve a level of completion incomprehensible to our egos. Perhaps this is what is meant in the gospel of Matthew:

He who finds his life will lose it, and he who loses his life for my sake will find it. (Matt. 10:39)

THE LOST ART OF SACRIFICE

BEWARE THE CULTURE OF "ME"

In many circles, sacrifice is considered a noose around our necks to prevent us from achieving our earthly desires. The world claims that any talk about sacrifice is a sign of oppression, of repression, of submission and subjugation. Consider a best-selling book called *The Success Principles: How to Get from Where You Are to Where You Want to Be,* by Jack Canfield, the co-creator of the famed Chicken Soup for the Soul series. Canfield doesn't mince words about the importance of placing self above all else.

Just read a few of these lines from *The Success Principles*:

> If you find yourself in a situation you don't like, either work to make it better or leave. Do something to change it or get the heck out. Agree to work on a relationship or get a divorce.[15]

> Not being clear about what you want and making other people's needs and desires more important than your own is simply a habit. You can break it by practicing the opposite habit.[16]

> How do you reconnect with your real passion? You start on the smallest level by honoring your preferences in every situation — no matter how large or small.[17]

People use these ideas to excuse decisions related to business, career, education, community, and even their most intimate

---

[15] Jack Canfield with Janet Switzer, *The Success Principles: How to Get from Where You Are to Where You Want to Be* (New York, HarperResource Books, 2005), 13.

[16] Ibid, 27.

[17] Ibid.

relationships. No matter the area of life, when we are so focused on our wants and needs that we can't see two feet in front of us, we are bound to wreak havoc not only on those around us but on ourselves as well.

THE FEEL-GOOD MENTALITY

It's interesting how we can find a way to justify our actions in order to follow our passions. Even more telling is how well we can rationalize them to the detriment of those around us. Maggie Gallagher, author of *The Abolition of Marriage*, talks of how we, as a culture, have begun to look inward, insisting on following our feelings, rather than making decisions that might entail sacrifice for love of others. She profiles Lindsey, a wife and mother who left her husband of six years for another man with whom she felt she shared more interests. Gallagher says Lindsey brooded for some time about how to end her relationship, knowing that her five-year-old daughter would be affected. "It took months for Lindsey to summon the courage to end her marriage. 'I'd say to myself, How can I do this to her?... Finally, though, I realized that she'd be much happier if I were happy.' (Funny how this magic formula never works in reverse. No one contemplating divorce ever looks at the child and says, 'I'll be happy only if she's happy.')"[18]

It's important to note that when we are at the center of our decision-making process, the entire Body of Christ suffers. God desires that we be sanctified through our vocation. That means that we can grow in holiness through the trials and challenges

---

[18] Maggie Gallagher, *The Abolition of Marriage: How We Destroy Lasting Love* (Washington, DC: Regnery, 1996), 217–218.

that we face in everyday life. Family members — especially those we love — can become crosses. But as Christians, we are called to carry those crosses with joy and gratitude, not to abandon them.

Sadly, many people in times of uncertainty or suffering choose to pursue their happiness to the detriment of those around them. If they think about God at all, they tell themselves that God loves them no matter what and that He wouldn't want them to suffer under this or that circumstance. And the culture condones this mentality, even celebrates it. The talk of the day is liberty and independence, personal choice and personal truth or satisfaction.

Our life decisions have a widespread ripple effect. Perhaps it's high time our culture considered the long-term effects of the laissez-faire social mentality we've created and began making personal choices that take into consideration how they might affect those around us.

I used the example of divorce because it is unfortunately so common. Of course, the Church teaches that there are some circumstances where separation is permitted, such as abuse or endangerment.[19] But, sadly, even when it comes to circumstances of our own design, such as the pursuit of personal fulfillment, financial success, or even a challenging struggle, our culture encourages us to make decisions with little or no consideration for those around us. We are told that the best decisions are all about ourselves and our immediate satisfaction — the world be damned.

Think of all the decisions that have become accepted and even celebrated by the world: divorce, abortion, single parenthood (as a choice), euthanasia, abandonment, drinking, drugs, obesity, gambling, debt, alternative lifestyles, extramarital affairs, pornography — as well as countless other choices. So often we

---

[19] See *Catechism of the Catholic Church* (CCC), nos. 1649–1650.

believe that in order to be happy, we need not sacrifice for the good of others. We need not deny ourselves what we want, and we are free to pursue our desires come what may. We are told that life is all about *my* happiness, *my* pleasure, *my* short-term gain. This is called the feel-good mentality, to borrow the toxic slogan of the sixties: if it feels good, do it.

The devil will do his best to manipulate our minds and hearts into going against God's law. And he pretty much has the culture under his thumb. Don't be swayed by his lies! Contrary to popular belief, life is not all about *me* (or you). It is not about finding *myself* in this life. It is not about what I want and what I think I need. Each and every one of us is called to give of ourselves, to love our neighbor, and to love God above all things.

In a Lenten reflection on "suffering love," Bishop Barron wrote,

> When a mother stays up all night, depriving herself of sleep, in order to care for a sick child, she is following this same example, suffering so that some of his suffering might be alleviated. When a person willingly bears an insult and refuses to fight back or return insult for insult, he is suffering for the sake of love.[20]

So much of our sacrifice is tied to our vocations. This chapter focused on the big picture using the example of divorce. But scenarios are infinitely diverse and could never be contained in the pages of one chapter on sacrifice. Regardless of your situation, it will be the culmination of moments like those mentioned

[20] "Suffering Love," reflection by Fr. Robert Barron, posted on Couples for Christ, June 10, 2014, https://www.couplesforchrist-global.org/articles.aspx?id=163.

by Bishop Barron that will make for long-term joy. We will be sanctified through our loving surrender in each and every one of those moments.

Maybe you read the above and think, "Sure. That sounds great. But it's just not realistic. Maybe I have no desire to be joyful about my situation." So pray for that desire. Pray that you might open your heart to whatever God has in store for your future. Second, you say, "Even if I had a desire, the pain is just too overwhelming." It may seem so today. But God is right there with you in your pain. His infinite compassion and mercy are there for you. Right now. But your ability to embrace it comes down to your willingness to surrender.

WHERE SELF MEETS SACRIFICE

When my son was five, he hated baths. I mean *hated* them. He could be as black as coal, with dirt caked in his hair, mud dripping off the soles of his feet and grime covering both of his hands; but if I suggested a bath, his response was always one of sheer desperation. "No, no, no!' He would plead, sobbing. "Not today — I'll do it tomorrow." The very concept of scrubbing himself clean was abhorrent to him. The entire process was excruciatingly painful, because he felt so completely exploited and victimized.

My then three-year-old, on the other hand, *loved* to be clean. She could hear the word *bath* whispered from three rooms away and would have her clothes off, diving into the tub before I could even turn on the water! She virtually purred when I scrubbed her hair, and she relished in the swish of the waves she created in the bubbles as she brushed her hands along the water's surface. The picture of perfect peace and contentment, she clearly basked in the knowledge that all the dirt would soon be washed away.

Same water. Same process. *Very* different attitude.

So do you abhor the situation you find yourself in today? Or do you lovingly accept it as a personal gift from the Divine Physician intended for your purification? Maybe baths aren't the greatest analogy for this discussion. After all, some of us love to swim, while some of us hate the water. But there is something to be said for our submission in the face of necessity. In other words, if the bath is going to happen either way, why not accept it? Or better yet, be grateful for it?

Sure, you say. But taking a bath is more of an inconvenience than an actual misfortune. True. But how many of our daily frustrations are mere inconveniences? I mean, most of the problems in my daily life are of the "first world" variety. Much-needed sleep interrupted by an early riser, messy kids, busy schedules, grumpy spouse, long lines … and the list goes on ad nauseum. Couldn't I approach each of these situations with rose-colored glasses? Wouldn't life be much more satisfying if I chose to be grateful for those things that I used to find annoying? How would my life change if I viewed the many demands of family life as God-given opportunities to grow in virtue?

Regarding His own life, Christ told Pilate, "No one takes it from me; but I lay it down of my own accord" (John 10:18). He was imprisoned, beaten, and forced to carry His Cross to His very death on Calvary. *But* not only did Christ accept His fate; He chose to embrace it as God's will. This powerful response in the face of unbelievable circumstances is a signal to us, His disciples.

In my own case, twenty years after watching *Mr. Holland's Opus*, I read a novel by Bess Streeter Aldrich, a writer from Nebraska who wrote in the early twentieth century about life in the pioneer days. *A Lantern in Her Hand* depicts the life story of Abbie Mackenzie. As a little girl and even a young woman,

Abbie has her heart set on becoming a singer. Full of talent, she is even offered the opportunity to achieve her dream; but she doesn't fall in love with the rich doctor who would move her to New York and possibly make her dreams come true. Instead, she falls head over heels for Will Deal, a young farmer who promises a life of love, albeit hardship, as they head West to homestead on the wild Nebraska prairie.

So even young ladies living in the 1800s had big dreams. Like Mr. Holland, Abbie never achieves the dream of her youth. Instead, she dies alone on her homestead, surrounded by the things she loves, after living a long but *beautiful* life full of trial and sacrifice with her husband and children.

Like *Mr. Holland's Opus*, this story struck close to home for me; but I watched it through a different lens. The fact is that my plans are not necessarily God's plans. And to become a saint requires me to unite my will with His—not to force my rectangular checklist of goals into the round hole of sanctity. No doubt God's plans for your life are more rewarding and more amazing than any you ever could have imagined for yourself: plans that include the surest and most direct path to Heaven—a path designed for you alone.

CULTIVATING THE ART OF SACRIFICE

Is there any situation in your life in which you find yourself rationalizing your decisions by telling yourself that your happiness is the "most" important consideration? Do you tell yourself that the Church doesn't know any better or is making unreasonable "demands" on you? If so, may I suggest that you find out what the Church actually teaches about your situation? Not what you think is the "rule" your choices are violating. Go deeper. Find out *why* the Church teaches what she does. Her reasons may surprise you and might even lead you to a place of healing that you hadn't thought possible.

Action

1. The greatest response to the lie of serving me, myself, and I is to turn your gaze away from yourself. The acronym JOY can remind you that joy is found by serving *Jesus* first, *others* second, and *yourself* third. Spend time in adoration today, prayerfully asking Our Lord to help you make your decisions in that order.

2. The world tells us to love ourselves. The Beatitudes call for us to love God. St. Bonaventure says, "We render ourselves subject to whatever we affectionately love; and therefore we ought to love nothing but him, because subjection to him is the only true liberty."[21] Read the Beatitudes today: Matthew 5:3–12. Pray that you will be inwardly transformed so that you will love as Christ loves.

Suggested Reading

The Hidden Power of Kindness, by Fr. Lawrence Lovasik
Marriage 911: How God Saved Our Marriage, by Greg and Julie Alexander, chapter 12

---

[21] *Saint Bonaventure's Life of Our Lord and Saviour Jesus Christ* (Lexington, KY: Christ the King Library, 2014), 152.

Contemplate the Cross

The Jews had the shadow without the reality,
the Christian possesses a truth hidden under veils,
the saint sees it face to face.
The Old Testament is manifested in the New
and the New shall be manifested in heaven.

—Abbe Gaume[22]

Have you ever focused your gaze upon a crucifix and contemplated its significance? Knowing that God could have chosen to save us through any other process imaginable (or even unimaginable), have you ever meditated upon the crude and gruesome means by which He actually chose to save us? Take a few minutes to examine a crucifix. Study, inch by ravaged inch, the limp, lifeless, bloodied body of Christ, hanging from the Cross. Look at the crown of thorns pressed down upon His precious head, piercing His skull from virtually every angle. Consider the solid and un-forgiving nature of the nails pounded savagely through His hands and feet. Ponder the indignity of Christ's hanging helplessly after

---

[22] Abbe Gaume, *Catechism of Perseverance* (N.p.: Christ the King Library, 2014), xxi–xxii.

having His clothing stripped roughly away from His body, already bloodied from the scourging with spiked whips that tore His flesh. On some crucifixes you will even notice the ironic juxtaposition of the gleaming rays of glory framing His pitiful head—a head that hangs heavily upon His chest in lifeless humiliation.

I have often found myself avoiding a close examination of the crucifix. As I avoid directly viewing a full eclipse of the sun to protect my eyes from harm, so, too, have I caught myself glancing at a crucifix only indirectly, in order to protect my heart from the graphic reality of the death suffered by God for my benefit. In fact, for years I had an aversion to the idea of Christ's death on the Cross.

No matter how hard we try to understand, no matter how long we continue to grapple with the Gospel message, the mystery of the Cross remains just that—a mystery. That there was a God who loved me made sense. That He wanted me to be with Him forever in Heaven made sense. Even that Adam and Eve thwarted the original plan made sense. I never grappled with the notion that our forefathers' actions could negatively affect us. That happens all the time. An alcoholic negatively impacts his children and, by virtue of that impact, can affect lives for generations. The same is true of divorce, poverty, education, and so forth. It makes sense that what is true of the particular would also apply at the aggregate level.

But the idea that God came down from Heaven; entered the world as a poor, helpless babe and lived a relatively hidden life until His thirtieth year; and stepped into the public square, surrounded Himself with devoted friends, walked with them, talked with them, and confided in them over the course of three years, only to allow leaders of the day to mock Him, scourge Him, strip Him of His dignity, nail Him to a cross in a most humiliating way, and leave Him to hang for three hours until He breathed His last?

That just didn't compute.

In all my wisdom, it seemed He didn't need to die, and certainly we didn't need to die to ourselves. Rather, we could all have just become one happy family, enjoying life on earth as we looked forward to Heaven together.

Think about it. Of all the plans that God could have conceived for our redemption, could He have possibly chosen one more peculiar than the one He chose?

What about that makes sense? I must admit that, as a Protestant, I didn't ask many questions. I just accepted that Christ died so I didn't have to.

But when I finally forced myself to examine the crucifix, I began to think I wasn't seeing the whole picture. I began asking questions. Thankfully, our Catholic Faith offers answers. And unlike the gruesome nature of the Cross, in typical Christian irony, the answers are more beautiful — and sensible — than I could have ever imagined.

WHY GOD HAD TO DIE

One thing that really helped me to make sense of Christ's sacrifice was a nifty little children's book that put everything into perspective. *Christopher's Talks to Catholic Children*, by David Greenstock, was first published in 1944. In the book, Christopher (Christ bearer) explains why Christ came down from Heaven and died on the Cross, so that we might have eternal life. He uses the analogy of insults and praise in the place of sin and reparation to clarify why God chose the means for our salvation that He did. Christopher begins by using an example of insults. He says that when one person insults another, the insult is considered more or less grave depending on the "level" of the person being insulted.

THE LOST ART OF SACRIFICE

To illustrate Greenstock's point, imagine that on a pilgrimage to Rome, you are blessed to be among a papal audience. Along with a multitude of other pilgrims, you make your way to St. Peter's Square with your camera ready, and all about you are whispers of hushed excitement. Finally, the moment arrives, and the pope rolls out in his little white popemobile, making his way through the crowd to the front of the throng, where you stand with your loved ones, all ready to greet him. Imagine that, as you say a brief prayer of thanksgiving, you see the pope step out of his vehicle and begin shaking hands with the persons near you. The person beside you steps forward toward the Holy Father. As you glance up, you are shocked as the man looks the pope right in the eye and shouts, loudly and clearly, "You are such an idiot!" Can you imagine the gasps that would emanate from every angle? (Yes, I realize that we now live in a world where that insult is relatively mild; but please humor me with the clean example. If it helps to insert your own version, please feel free.)

Now, imagine if you heard your daughter say those same words to her little brother. Of course, as a child of God, your son shares the same dignity as the pope. And of course, those words would be wrong, no matter who the recipient is. But would there be the same shock? The same outrage? The same level of disbelief? No. Because the level of insult depends on the level of the person being insulted. In today's anti-authority culture, perhaps there are some who would disagree with this point; but throughout history, there has been some element of consideration and respect due to figures of authority; and who on earth would deserve more consideration and respect than the Vicar of Christ, our spiritual father?

Or, consider the opposite scenario — the power of praise. Imagine you work in a call center with hundreds of other people.

Orderly rows of cubicles create a maze through a giant warehouse of space, and you make your way to your tiny corner every day, ready to hop on the phone and dial away. One day, a colleague peeks around the corner of your partition and says, "Hey, you're doing a great job—keep up the good work." How would that make you feel? Pretty good, right? But then imagine that the next day, as you make call after call, you begin to hear a buzz of excitement around you. You look over the makeshift wall that separates you from your neighbor and give him a questioning look before your supervisor walks up, clearly looking for you. "Would you mind following me? The CEO would like to speak with you in his office," she says. "The CEO?" you think. "What did I do wrong?" Heart racing, you grab your belongings and follow the supervisor all the way through the maze and up the stairs to the office of the CEO, feeling the eyes of your colleagues on your back as you go. When you arrive, the CEO smiles in welcome, opens the door wide, and gestures for you to have a seat in the plush leather chair across from his desk. He makes his way around, sits to face you, and—still smiling—leans forward and says, "I called you up here because I've been looking at your numbers. I have to tell you, you are really doing a great job. Keep up the good work!"

Which of those compliments—the one from your colleague or the one from the CEO of your company—would you consider to be the greater one? No doubt the one from the CEO. Why? Because, unlike the level of insult, which is more or less grave depending on the level of the person *being insulted*, the level of a compliment depends on the level of the person *giving* the praise.

In order for an insult to be rectified, the person being insulted must be praised by a person of the same or a higher level.

In the case of Original Sin (and all sin from that day to this), the sin was all the more horrible because it was committed against

God—the receiver of the "insult" being of infinite greatness. Because the insult was infinitely great, as the person insulted was infinitely great, there was nothing we could do, no matter how much we tried to make things right. No matter how much we repented or how much we were willing to offer, human beings could never "make it right" enough to reach the level of the sin committed, since a compliment extended by man can never overcome an insult committed against God.

That said, the sin was committed by man; therefore, a man had to make reparation. On the other hand, there is no man who could qualify as high enough to make up for the level of the sin committed against God. So only someone at the level of God could make up for the sin man committed against God.

So He did it. God condescended to come down to earth and take on the nature of man in the Person of Christ. He took on sin, carried it upon His shoulders—all sin ever committed—so that once and for all, He could offer Himself up in expiation for that sin. By sin, man had revolted against God; our Lord humbled Himself before God, even unto death. By sin, man had offended infinite justice; our Lord suffered all that a man can suffer, and in a manner infinitely meritorious, since He is God and man.[23]

Finally, the Person offering reparation was on equal footing with the Person who had been insulted. And why such a gruesome death? No other means of execution would have been proportionate to the extreme gravity of our condition under sin. Never think for one minute that the mode of Christ's death was random. According to the *Catechism*, "Jesus' violent death was not the result of chance in an unfortunate coincidence of circumstances, but is part of the mystery of God's plan" (599).

---

[23] Gaume, *Catechism of Perseverance*, 168–169.

By the merits of His sacrifice, Christ reopened the gates of Heaven for each and every one of us, none of whom could possibly have accomplished the feat without Him. This opening of the gates of Heaven was the restoration of the relationship between God and man, which had been destroyed by our first parents, Adam and Eve. Christ came that we might have life (John 10:10). In the end, His death on the Cross is not gruesome, but beautiful, for He offered Himself from the depths of His being—He gave everything—that we might receive everything.

And the story doesn't end here. Christ offers us eternity; but He will not force it upon us. We were once united to the First Adam, but Christ—the Second Adam—came that we might unite ourselves with Him. In so doing, we secure our place with Him in eternity, rendering forever what was lost at the start.

CULTIVATING THE ART OF SACRIFICE

A crucifix can be a stark reminder of the evils in the world and of the great challenges found in life. But more than that, it is a beautiful sign of hope and a solid example that love conquers all things—even death.

Action

1. Spend five minutes today looking at a crucifix. Meditate on its meaning and how the Cross has manifested itself in your life. Can you take any lessons from Christ on how to approach your own challenges?
2. Read the following lessons on sacrifice. Meditate on what the Old Testament teaches us about sacrifice and how

these sacrifices are fulfilled by Jesus on the Cross. Don't feel that you have to read them all at once, but as time allows.

Lessons on Sacrifice from the Old Testament

Old Testament stories also offer lessons in the art of sacrifice. We can think of them as rungs on a ladder leading to the perfect sacrifice of Christ, through which all things are made new. As we make our way to the top, we must make use of each rung in order to maintain solid footing. Without squarely securing our footing, we risk toppling from the ladder.

These sacrifices were each meant in their own ways to reveal some truth about the sacrifice that Our Lord asks of each of us. Whether founded on obedience, gratitude, trust, love, faithfulness, unity of will, or acknowledgment of God's ultimate supremacy, our sacrifices begin with *the* sacrifice. Our crosses all begin with *the* Cross.

1. Read Genesis 4:1–16 about Abel: first and foremost, a sacrifice requires a firm recognition of the sovereignty of God and our proper relationship to Him. He created all things and controls all things, ruling all with supreme wisdom.

2. Read Genesis 6:5 — 9:17 about Noah: in the knowledge of God's transcendent authority, we must trust in His providence, being ever thankful for His grace and mercy.

3. Read Genesis 22:1–19 about Abraham: in that trust and thanksgiving, we can obey God with full confidence, loving Him above all things with the knowledge that He is our first beginning and our final end.

4. Read Exodus 12:1–28 about the Passover: through that obedience, we can accept the reality of the Body of Christ, the union of all her members with Christ as the head, with the hope of an eternal union in Heaven as one Body, united as Christ is united with the Father.

5. Read 1 Kings 18:17–39 about Elijah: this hope in God's love and mercy is reflected in our sacrifices of faith, our prayer of trustful surrender to divine providence, and a penchant for adoration of a God who is all good, all merciful and all powerful.

6. Read 2 Maccabees 7:1–41 about seven brothers and their mother: finally, that surrender can lead us, as it led the widow and her seven sons, to absolute martyrdom, a complete surrender of our wills, our desires, our wants and needs, even our very lives, to a God in whom we have placed all our confidence, all our hopes, all our dreams, and all our trust.

As we climb that ladder, we approach our heavenly abode, traveling from rung to rung all the way to the foot of the Cross. In all our humility and trust, Christ Himself can lift us up, easing the pain of our cross, carrying us to Heaven through His ultimate sacrifice and our union with Him.

Suggested Reading

Life of Christ, by Fulton J. Sheen
Jesus of Nazareth: The Story of His Life Simply Told, by Mother Mary of Loyola

5

Become One with Christ

I have been crucified with Christ;
it is no longer I who live, but Christ who lives in me;
and the life I now live in the flesh I live by faith in the
Son of God, who loved me and gave himself for me.

—Galatians 2:20

In 1889, one hundred years after the Age of Enlightenment ravaged Paris, Elisabeth Arrighi, a young Catholic woman born and
raised in that beautiful city, fell in love with and married Felix
Leseur, a man who had embraced the tenets of atheism, hook,
line, and sinker. Felix, a lapsed Catholic and a doctor, made
it his life's work to spread the lies of materialism, even to the
point of pressuring his wife to dismiss her Faith and join him in
the "rational" world, where science reigned supreme and faith
was mere superstition held by only the naïve and the ignorant.

How many of us find ourselves in Elisabeth's situation? Someone we love has left the Church and boldly mocks or tries to
undermine our faith? How many of us look out into our communities or out into the broader environment and feel alone as
Christians in a godless world? The numbers are growing for sure.

Thankfully, we can learn much from Elisabeth Leseur's experience. Her husband almost succeeded in driving a wedge between
her and God forever. But God had other plans.

A few years into their marriage, Elisabeth began to pray for
the conversion of her husband. She never tried to argue him to
conversion, but, rather, practiced her Faith in isolation, while
offering all her prayers, trials, tribulations, sufferings, and even
her very life for this purpose.[24] In her diary, Elisabeth logged
her suffering and her secret desires for the loved ones in her
life — especially for Felix:

> December 1910: May Thy blessed hands help me to carry,
> and may Thy love and the close union of Thy heart with
> mine sweeten this unhappy solitude of mine. Let this soli-
> tude come to an end one day when, by Thy grace, Thou
> shalt convert and sanctify those near and dear persons
> whom I implore Thee to make Christians and apostles,
> O Jesus Christ, my Lord and my God![25]

Elisabeth suffered from many health problems. Soon after she
and Felix were married, she suffered from an intestinal abscess,
from which she never completely recovered.[26] In 1907, she suffered from liver problems and was virtually bedridden. In 1911,
she had a cancerous tumor removed from her breast. Through all
this time, she joyfully offered her sufferings in union with Christ
for the conversion of her husband and others who may not yet
have known Christ. Just before the surgery to remove the tumor,
Elisabeth offered her life for her husband's conversion:

[24] *The Secret Diary of Elisabeth Leseur*, xiii.
[25] Ibid., 99.
[26] Ibid., ix.

April 9, 1911: An intimate compact between my soul and God, my heart and the heart of Jesus, through the intercession of the Blessed Virgin and under the protection of St. Joseph and St. Teresa. Confidence this time of being heard again. Now, O Lord, I await the fulfillment of Thy blessed promises, and I wish to receive faithfully what they bring me in Thy name. May God be blessed![27]

We speak often of the gift of redemption that Christ offers us via His death on the Cross. But through His Passion and death, He gives us another gift as well, one that we often overlook. He offers us an opportunity to experience firsthand that "greater love" of which He speaks — not through His sacrifice but through our own. Each and every one of us is called to unite our sacrifices, our sufferings, to Christ's sacrifice on the Cross.

Elisabeth understood this gift and lived it out throughout the course of her marriage. Her diary inspires us to live holy lives joyfully in the face of suffering and loneliness:

1912: Union with Jesus Christ, which we shall realize in Heaven in joy and vision, is already possible for us on earth in suffering. That is why all souls in love with Jesus, those souls that have heard the mysterious and irresistible call of Christ, love suffering and, far from rejecting it with an entirely human horror, ask for it, desire it as the sweet forerunner of the Master, as that which ushers us into His presence. It is suffering that reveals the Cross to us, that opens the divine Heart to us, that enables us to enter into this supernatural world that no human thing can reach, which we will know only in eternity, but from which a

---

[27] Ibid., 106.

glimmer shines over us through the grace of suffering and the radiance of the Cross.[28]

In this life, we are called to unite our sufferings to Christ's sufferings, our love to His love, our wills to His holy will, our lives to His life, and our deaths — even in those moments when we choose to die to ourselves in spirit or deed for the good of another — to His death on the Cross.

THE BODY OF CHRIST

When Elisabeth offered her suffering for the conversion and salvation of others, she demonstrated understanding of a critical truth about the world that seems to have been lost or minimized in recent generations. Elisabeth recognized that the "Church is both visible and *spiritual, a hierarchical society and the Mystical Body of Christ.*"[29] As part of His Body, we are as intimately connected to our neighbors as our arms are connected to our hands, or our legs to our feet. In other words, our prayers, acts of penance, mortification, and other sacrifices can and do have a direct effect on those around us because we are indeed one body. Just as the food ingested by the mouth nourishes the blood flowing through our veins, a sacrifice made in love has a direct effect on the Body of Christ.

This is not some obscure, analogous concept. The Body of Christ is mentioned several times in the New Testament. St. Paul describes it:

> For just as the body is one and has many members, and all the members of the body, though many, are one body,

---

[28] Ibid., 110.
[29] CCC 779

so it is with Christ. For by one Spirit we were all baptized into one body — Jews or Greeks, slaves or free — and all were made to drink of one Spirit. (1 Cor. 12:12–13)

The Church is made up of many individuals, just as the body is made of many cells; all are incorporated into the one Body under Christ:

He is the image of the invisible God, the first-born of all creation; for in him all things were created, in heaven and on earth, visible and invisible, whether thrones or dominions or principalities or authorities — all things were created through him and for him. He is before all things, and in him all things hold together. He is the head of the body, the church. (Col. 1:15–18)

And this Body is not limited to our friends and neighbors here on earth but includes all those, living and dead, in Heaven, in Purgatory, and on earth:

"We believe in the communion of all the faithful of Christ, those who are pilgrims on earth, the dead who are being purified, and the blessed in heaven, all together forming one Church; and we believe that in this communion, the merciful love of God and his saints is always [attentive] to our prayers" (Paul VI, CPG § 30). (CCC 962)

One important point that we must keep in mind is that Christ is the head not only of baptized Christians but of all mankind, for, according to Archbishop Fulton Sheen, "those who are unbaptized, though not actually in the Church, are in the Church potentially. And this potentiality is rooted in two things — first and principally the power of Christ which is sufficient for the salvation of the whole human race, and secondly in free will."[30]

This means that all our prayers, works, joys and sufferings can be offered for all the living and also for the suffering souls in Purgatory, who desperately need our prayers. (The saints in Heaven have no need of prayers, but we can rest assured that they certainly pray for us!)

THE IMPORTANCE OF THE MYSTICAL

When we recognize the intimate relationship between our own souls and each and every other soul that makes up the Body of Christ, we can see the potential consequences of our actions. When I offer myself in any way for the good of another out of love, I also help myself. Consider the analogy of the human body. In one who has lost his sight, does not his hearing serve to make up for the loss? When one is in a wheelchair, do not his arms become stronger, aiding his body in ways that his legs no longer can? Every part of the body serves the body as a whole. And giving oneself for the good of another serves the Body of Christ as a whole as well. As such, it serves the one who offers himself.

Conversely, when I pursue my own interests to the exclusion of others, I destroy my very self because I infect the Body of Christ with a perversion of truth. And this self-interest affects every area of my life (and the lives of those I meet) in a destructive way.

A recognition of the importance of the mystical is severely lacking in the world today. Our experience in the world can stunt our growth, preventing us from moving much beyond infancy.

---

[30] Fulton J. Sheen, *The Mystical Body of Christ* (Notre Dame: Christian Classics, 2015), 303n4.

Because he is only *self*-aware, a baby insists on the immediate satisfaction of his every need. He cries when he is wet, hungry, tired, or uncomfortable, giving no thought to how he might be infringing on the needs or plans of others. The process of growing up involves moving beyond our limited infantile perception. But all the worldly focus on immediate gratification and self-satisfaction discourages us from seeing beyond our own desires. As a result, our spiritual lives are often stunted in adolescence and can remain there throughout adulthood.

SERVING THE BODY OF CHRIST THROUGH SACRIFICE

So how do we begin to direct our attention outward—raising our eyes toward others and away from ourselves? As demonstrated by Elisabeth Leseur, we have the opportunity, through our participation in the Body of Christ, to unite our suffering with His, to offer acts of self-denial, to offer all our prayers, works, joys, and sufferings, as the Morning Offering so eloquently says. As one body in Christ, our union is not a mere concept or a symbol. Rather, the very gift of self that Christ has given us is the grace that helps us to love as He loves. As St. Paul explains, through our participation in the Body, we have the privilege of participating in redemption: "Now I rejoice in my sufferings for your sake, and in my flesh I complete what is lacking in Christ's afflictions for the sake of his body, that is, the church" (Col. 1:24). Paul bids us to offer ourselves as well, to worship God through our participation in this new concept of sacrifice that Jesus has introduced by the Cross: "I appeal to you therefore, brethren, by the mercies of God, to present your bodies as a living sacrifice, holy and acceptable to God, which is your spiritual worship" (Rom. 12:1).

But why? Why should we rejoice in suffering? Why should we offer our very selves as a living sacrifice to God? Is this some twisted call for masochism or self-destruction?

On the contrary.

BRINGING MEANING TO OUR PAIN

As we look beyond our immediate situation, we can begin to see the overwhelming power our crosses can wield in the world. The truth is that we have been given a profound opportunity to serve the Body of Christ, and therefore ourselves, through the Cross. Through our union with Christ on the Cross, God has blessed us with the opportunity to participate with Christ in the Redemption.

To be able to suffer with Christ is an extraordinary blessing. According to St. Teresa of Calcutta,

> Sorrow, suffering ... is but a kiss of Jesus—a sign that you have come so close to Jesus that He can kiss you. —I think this is the most beautiful definition of suffering. —So let us be happy when Jesus stoops down to kiss us. —I hope we are close enough that He can do it.[31]

To suffer with Christ is indeed a gift. But to offer that suffering to Christ for the salvation of souls—that is the ultimate in charity. This is known as *redemptive suffering*, which we'll talk more about in chapter 8.

---

[31] Mother Teresa, *Come Be My Light: The Private Writings of the Saint of Calcutta*, ed. Brian Kolodiejchuk (New York: Doubleday, 2007), 281.

Many who lack understanding laugh when they hear the old saying "Offer it up." They roll their eyes. "Those Catholics, thinking they can earn their way to Heaven!"

But this is *not* what Catholics think!

> On the cross Christ took upon himself the whole weight of evil and took away the "sin of the world" (Jn 1:29; cf. Isa 53:4–6), of which illness is only a consequence. By his passion and death on the cross Christ has given new meaning to suffering; it can henceforth configure us to him and unite us with his redemptive Passion. (CCC 1505)

In our own pain, we have the sacrament of the Anointing of the Sick to enable us, through the grace of God, to unite our sufferings more intimately with Christ on the Cross:

> By the grace of this sacrament the sick person receives the strength and the gift of uniting himself more closely to Christ's Passion: in a certain way he is consecrated to bear fruit by configuration to the Savior's redemptive Passion. Suffering, a consequence of original sin, acquires a new meaning; it becomes a participation in the saving work of Jesus. (CCC 1521)

There is no earning here. There is only cooperation. Through His death on the Cross, Christ provided an example for us to follow:

> A new commandment I give to you, that you love one another; even as I have loved you, that you also love one another. By this all men will know you are my disciples, if you have love for one another. (John 13:34–35)

With those six little words, "even as I have loved you," Christ gives us everything.

Love is not a pile of sentimental poems or a confetti of rose petals streaming from the heavens. In reality, love looks a lot like suffering. It can be painful. It can be heart-wrenching. Indeed, love is a sacrifice — a sacrifice first wrought by Christ, who came to show us the Way.

First Christ defined love. And then He asked us to practice it: "You shall love the Lord your God with all your heart, and with all your soul, and with all your mind. This is the great and first commandment. And a second is like it, You shall love your neighbor as yourself" (Matt. 22:37–39).

For God, love equals sacrifice.

And what is a sacrifice but suffering, wrapped in a beautiful package and offered as a pure gift? Elisabeth Leseur certainly understood that. And her efforts wrought much fruit. Upon her death, her husband, Felix, not only returned to his Catholic Faith but also became a Dominican priest! And he spent much time publishing Elisabeth's writings and was instrumental in initiating the cause for her canonization. Although he has since passed, his efforts are still underway. At this time, Elisabeth Leseur is considered a Servant of God.

CULTIVATING THE ART OF SACRIFICE

Prayerfully ask the Holy Spirit to guide you on this journey toward a more fruitful life filled with the joy of loving sacrifice.

Action

If you aren't already in the habit of praying a morning offering, consider adding it to your routine. As you get out of bed each morning, kneel at your bedside and offer your entire day to your Heavenly Father. A morning offering can be as simple as saying, "Jesus, I give you my day." There are countless variations of the prayer, but below is a traditional version that my family adopted:

O Jesus, through the Immaculate Heart of Mary, I offer You my prayers, works, joys, and sufferings of this day in union with the Holy Sacrifice of the Mass throughout the world. I offer them for all the intentions of your Sacred Heart: the salvation of souls, reparation for sin, and the reunion of all Christians. I offer them for the intention of our bishops and of all apostles of prayer, and in particular for those recommended by our Holy Father this month. Amen.

Suggested Reading

The Secret Diary of Elisabeth Leseur, by Elisabeth Leseur
The Mystical Body of Christ, by Fulton J. Sheen

Part 2

Avoiding Satan's Traps

He was a murderer from the beginning, and has
nothing to do with the truth, because there is no truth
in him. When he lies, he speaks according to his own
nature, for he is a liar and the father of lies.

—John 8:44

We have in our path a formative opponent whose sole objective is to ensure that we do not achieve our goal of perfect union with God. It is the devil's mission to keep us forever separated from God: "Then the dragon was angry with the woman, and went off to make war on the rest of her offspring, on those who keep the commandments of God and bear testimony to Jesus" (Rev. 12:17). Despite knowing there is a traitor in our midst, we Christians find ourselves falling for his lies, one after another. The devil will always do his best to separate sacrifice from its true end, which is worship, honor, respect, love — God. The devil is nothing if not cunning and subtle, but his only goal is to separate and destroy, which makes it all the more critical that we be wary of his lies.

6

Beware the Traps of Modernism: Lies about Spiritual Traditions

Were one to attempt the task of collecting together all the errors that have been broached against the faith and to concentrate the sap and substance of them all into one, he could not better succeed than the Modernists have done.... As we have already intimated, their system means the destruction not of the Catholic religion alone but of all religion.

—Pope Pius X, *Pascendi Dominici Gregis* 39

Almost twenty years ago, I came upon *An Introduction to the Devout Life*, by St. Francis de Sales. The wisdom of St. Francis de Sales awakened my heart to the existence of a God who deserved my undying devotion. Until then, I had been a Catholic by choice. I was an intellectual convert who had weighed the evidence and acknowledged that the Catholic Church was the one true Church established by Christ and worthy of my obedience. I was excited by my knowledge of God but hadn't yet experienced His love for me. I had no concept of the "devout" life, other than through my contact with certain individuals in whom I had witnessed a supernatural spark that I began to crave.

An Introduction to the Devout Life opened for me an entirely new world, inspiring me to fall head over heels in love with Christ! I couldn't get enough time with Him. Suddenly prayer became a powerful presence in my life. Adoration was no longer boring but the fulfillment of a need so deep that I came away from it feeling refreshed and at peace. My faith was no longer a "duty" but a joy. I learned, as St. Paul advises, to "pray without ceasing" (1 Thess. 5:17, NRSV). For the most part, I lived in a state of gratitude. Had I been asked to give my life for my Lord, I can say with certainty that I would have been honored. Even my decision to homeschool my children was a direct result of reading this book because I imagined our school time spent learning, loving, and living the lives God desired for us, together as a family.

But time has a predictable way of passing, and I'm humbled to share that the springtime of my soul, which had been so lovely, slowly faded into late fall — dark and cool — bearing little of its former beauty.

It all began with what I thought was an inconsequential decision. A few years into my fervor, I decided to start rising thirty minutes later and give up my early-morning prayer time for some much-needed sleep. I had assumed I could find time later in the day for prayer (an impossible goal). Shortly thereafter, I decided one Tuesday that we shouldn't attend Mass that day because I had too much to do. A few days later, after staying up late the night before, I decided that wrestling with five little ones under nine during daily Mass would require too much energy. And so it went. Day by day, hour by hour, minute by minute, my prayer life slowly receded behind all those earthly obligations, frustrations, and escapes.

That passionate fire once lit by the Holy Spirit smoldered quietly as I barreled through my days. I was quite certain that something needed to change, but I lacked the will to make the time. It was much easier to avoid that longing by embracing various substitutions for our former relationship. I didn't do *bad* things. In fact, I continued to spend my free time teaching my children about God, reading books on theology, and watching movies about the saints. I knew all along that I should find time to spend *with* God, but I was trapped among my pressing and "easily accessible" substitutes.

Gradually, my life of "devotion" began to ring hollow. I viewed others who were living more worldly lifestyles with jealousy. While my husband and I struggled financially because we had renounced debt, friends and family members who had chosen to have two incomes and fewer kids seemed to live lavishly, purchasing new cars, taking annual vacations, and frequently eating out. I had friends who weren't struggling to take five young children to Mass every Sunday morning (much less *every* morning) who had never tried to fit Confession into Saturday schedules filled with kids' activities and entertainment. From the outside looking in, they didn't seem too concerned about what their children were watching, what kinds of games they were playing, or what music they listened to on their iPods (which, by the way, also had unlimited Internet access). Yet their children seemed to be doing great. Somewhere along the line, living for Christ became *hard*.

Slowly but surely, I began to feel like a martyr (meaning in a grudging and negative way), sluggishly making my way through life, viewing my days as a series of endless chores that I "should do" rather than the acts of love they had been at one time. I began to live like one wearing shackles, rather than one who is *free*.

Where had I gone wrong? It may seem obvious, but it took me a while to realize the cause of my troubles.

I had turned my eyes away from Christ. Like Peter, who took his eyes off our Lord and began to waver as he felt the wind (Matt. 14:28–30), I glanced away and began to waver as well.

I've realized that devotion is not merely a matter of walking the walk. Without much-needed grace gained through prayer and the sacraments, we lack the *will* necessary to train our eyes on Christ. As a result, it's only a matter of time before our eyes begin to wander.

Mother Mary Loyola addresses waning passion in her book *First Communion*. I can attest to her assertions:

> The devil has no chance with the fervent. So he tries to cool their fervour by getting them to be careless about prayer and the sacraments. This done, the way is open to him and he begins to attack them by all sorts of temptations. We are not ignorant of his plans, and as to be forewarned is to be forearmed, we must lay this up in our memory for our whole lifetime — that all falls from fervour begin by a neglect of prayer. A more useful piece of knowledge we could scarcely have.[32]

Once I reestablished my prayer life, things changed. My eyes returned to Christ, and my sacrifices once again became gifts of love, as opposed to shackles and chains. That doesn't mean those gifts are always my first choice at the moment, as when I have played board games with my kids despite having a strong desire to work or clean. Acts of love are not always the first desire we have in our hearts. Instead, they are acts of the will that we perform because of our love. And the fruits are endless.

Most of us have tons of demands on our time every day. We have families, careers, and community and household obligations. We can and often do get wrapped up in the physical world. It

---

[32] Mother Mary of Loyola, *First Communion* (Lisle, IL: St. Augustine Academy Press, 2011), 229.

becomes easy to overlook God, who waits silently for us. He waits patiently for us to realize that all those worldly obligations have meaning only when centered on Him. The spiritual life is that aspect of ourselves that forms a bond with Christ. The deeper the spiritual life, the stronger the bond, and the more peace and joy we can find in this world, whatever our circumstances.

The attractions of the world make it easy to forget that the most important things in this life are invisible: the Holy Trinity, the communion of saints, the efficacy of the sacraments, our souls and their state of grace, and Heaven. Although we may know these truths implicitly, *living* them presents a difficult challenge. Unfortunately, the challenge is made all the greater by the advance of modernism in the world.

MODERNISM IS A LIE

Satan has been successfully spreading the lie of modernism for centuries, and in recent generations he seems to be winning. The lie of *modernism*, which places man in the position that rightly belongs to God, dismisses the value of the spiritual and encourages us to keep our eyes and ears on what we can see and achieve in this life. It implicitly denies our need for salvation and ultimately looks to science as the new "god," through which man, himself, can save the world. We have allowed the lie of modernism to make its way into every nook and cranny of society—even into the practice of our Faith.

We see the effects of modernism in society and even in the Church—whether it is a call to a humanitarianism without mention of God, or a separation of science from religion, or a veritable dismissal of the necessity for the sacraments and for prayer. In 2020, because of the COVID-19 pandemic restrictions, we watched as churches were shut down in city after city while very few bishops defended our right to the sacraments. The message sent to the faithful, whether intentional or not, was that the body is more important than the soul. That is one recent example of modernism seeping into the Church.

In the article "Introduction to the Modernist Heresy: Why Modernism is Perilous," S. M. Miranda discusses some of the greatest threats to the Catholic Church today, including the dangers of modernism:

> Rather than attack the doctrines of God openly like previous heresies, modernism simply distracts the modern man by offering the allure of materialism. For example, instead of flatly denying the existence of God with philosophical arguments, moderns learn to embrace agnosticism by asserting that religion is not as important as other things in life like patriotism or "making a better world for our children." ... The charge of superstition is often levied on religion with little reasoning or argument from the modernist. It is simply a blanket statement that frees the modernist from the burden of belief in angels, demons and especially the inconvenient belief in hell. In the final analysis modernism seeks to kill the Church not by open warfare, but by drowning out her voice with the allure of hedonism, the frenetic hum of the freeways, the ring of the stock market, and the drone of the work place.[33]

---

[33] S. M. Miranda, "Introduction to the Modernist Heresy: Why Modernism is Perilous," St. Thomas Aquinas Forum, http://www.saintaquinas.com/modernism_intro.html.

Combine the overwhelmingly tantalizing draw of modernism with the lack of understanding among Catholics about the beauty and power found in the spiritual practices of our Faith, and you have what we face today—a mass exodus of the Church and a significant portion of practicing Catholics who are attached by a tenuous thread of commitment.

WITHOUT MEANING, FAITH SUFFERS

So how did Catholics go from virtually 100 percent participation in Mass and deep commitment to prayer and the spiritual life, to less than 25 percent participation in Mass and minuscule belief in the Real Presence, in miracles, in intercessory prayer, and in the power of the sacraments? While the sources of modernism are virtually unlimited and its affects far-reaching, perhaps my experience can provide a glimpse into one contributing factor.

Shortly before I converted to the Catholic Faith, my husband (fiancé at the time) lost one of his close friends in a car accident. I traveled with him to a small, predominantly Catholic town in northeast Nebraska for the funeral.

In my Protestant experience, the night before a funeral had been a time for people to get together (often in the funeral home) and celebrate the life of the deceased. Family members and friends would come to offer support and to pay respects by viewing the body; afterward they would take turns standing up before the congregation and speak about happier times when they had been with this special person whose loss they were now mourning.

Although I later learned that, in a Catholic church, this event is also called a wake or a visitation, everyone in this small town in Nebraska, as well as my husband's family, called it the Rosary. "Are you going to the Rosary?" they'd ask. "What time is the Rosary?" When we arrived, there was time to pay respects to the body and offer condolences, but the focus was on the prayers of the vigil, not on reminiscing. Shortly after we arrived, vigil prayers were said for the soul of the deceased, and then all of a sudden, everyone knelt quietly in their pews, holding beads in their hands, prepared to pray the Rosary at the conclusion of the vigil. Until then, I had never prayed a Rosary. In fact, I don't know if I had ever heard of a Rosary. And—God forgive me for saying this—as I looked around at all those people kneeling and chanting back to the leader in unison, "Holy Mary, Mother of God ...," I honestly thought, "What in the world am I getting myself into? This feels like something you would do in a cult!" Afterward, I said as much to my then fiancé, and he just laughed. He said he had never thought about it before; that's just what you did when someone died. Somehow that didn't make me feel any better.

My husband grew up knowing that his parents prayed the Rosary together every morning. He knew that they prayed it every Monday night when they went to their weekly Holy Hour. He'd tell me that sometimes, when one of the kids stayed home sick from school, it was a special privilege for them to be able to join Mom and Dad in praying their morning Rosary. His parents never discussed *why* the Rosary was prayed or what it meant. They just did it. Most likely that is the case with many Catholics from previous generations. They practiced their Faith. But the whys and wherefores were often not passed on. And so, many traditions have been forgotten or left by the wayside as the children of those Catholics moved into adulthood.

It wasn't until many years after that funeral that I began to understand the meaning of and power of the Rosary. Unfortunately, as I read my way into the Church and began to appreciate the beauty of this prayer and other Catholic devotions and practices and of the sacraments, I noticed that many in the Church had become more and more apt to dismiss them. In fact, through the years, I've been shocked at how many who hear I am a convert tell me, "I used to be Catholic, too."

Apparently, my experience is not uncommon. For those in the broader culture, as I was so many years ago, devotions are not only confusing; they are unsettling, making you feel a bit like being a room where everyone is speaking a language that you don't understand. The experience can leave you feeling uncomfortable and out of place. Even those with good intentions can come away from sacraments, prayers, or devotions feeling as if nothing has changed. As such, there has been much antipathy toward spiritual practices. Rather than demonstrate any sort of reverence or regard because they represent some characteristic of faith, the world, more often than not, chastises, disgraces, and shames those who lead lives of devotion. Even when subtle, this antipathy is bound to wear on us over time.

Many Catholics all but give up. First, they suffer from not having been taught the meaning of the spiritual, the reasons for all the practices and devotions they hear about in the Church; and on top of that, they have the broader, modernist, secular culture breathing down their necks, decrying the spiritual, taunting them, raising questions that Catholics can't answer. Over time, that constant dogging about our faith practices, the ever-present nature of the material world, the demands on daily life, the silence of God, and the confusion about all things spiritual have caused Catholics to lose appreciation for the most important aspect of our Faith: God's very intimate, mystical relationship to us through His Church.

THE SPIRITUAL IS WHERE IT'S AT

Without an appreciation for the power of the sacraments, especially the Eucharist, people see all that "stuff" as a multitude of obligations and baggage that have little to do with God. In that respect, they begin to wonder, "Why should I stay in a Church that asks something of me?" If Catholics don't understand the benefit of the material toward the achievement of the spiritual, if they don't accept or understand the spiritual authority of the Church as ordained by Christ and governed through the Holy Spirit, why would they be willing to follow all these arbitrary "man-made rules," as the culture calls them? Even for Catholics who seek to understand their Faith, it is easier to learn theology or to read about the saints than to practice various devotions the saints espoused, so they give in to outside pressure to abandon Catholic traditions.

Even those who believe in God and have no intention of leaving the Church ask questions — not with the intention of getting answers, but in a rhetorical fashion that allows them to neglect the gifts set before them by their Savior: Why must I attend Mass weekly if I don't get anything out of it? Why confess my sins to a priest when I can speak to God directly or, better yet, discuss my problems with a licensed psychologist? Why ask the saints for intercession? Why pray the Rosary? Of what value is fasting, and why in the world would I fast unless I wanted to lose weight?

Such questions and ideas stem from a lack of appreciation for a world that we cannot see but that nonetheless exists and provides for us an abundance of life that the physical world cannot possibly supply. The notion of sacrifice is rooted deeply in what we call our interior life, which deals with the state of the soul and its relationship to our Creator.

This gets us to the nature of the soul.

God communicates with each one of us through the natural world, yes, but also in a deep and profound way through the supernatural life of the soul, which he fills with His grace. If, through His grace, we obtain Heaven, then we will have achieved our highest end. But in the meantime, as we make our way through this life, we are meant to prepare ourselves for that eternity by growing in faith and uniting ourselves to Christ. We do this through the means God has provided for us: the sacraments, particularly the Holy Eucharist; prayers, including the Rosary; and traditional devotions such as those associated with the Sacred Heart of Jesus and the Immaculate Heart of Mary.

The spiritual life is something that must be *lived*. It is not stagnant, but organic and free, an interior vitality that can grow and blossom, provided it is effectively nourished. And because the spiritual life is *lived out*, it can be visibly observed through its fruits. As such, we can learn from the countless examples of how it has been lived out by others through the biographies and writings of the saints.

Perseverance is the driving force of discipline. Discipline is the driving force behind our holiness. We might wander into sin. But we'll never wander into holiness. We make choices every moment of every day. And most of them will involve sacrifice. We need to remember that each and every one of our sacrifices must be offered out of love. We must not simply go through the motions. Instead, we must recognize union with God as the particular motivation and end for every thought, word, and action. It may take much trial and error to persevere, but it will be worth it.

THE LOST ART OF SACRIFICE

WHAT KIND OF HOSPITAL IS THIS?

Sometimes we get bogged down in the practice of our Faith. We look to our left and to our right, and along with the culture, we see that, for other Christians, its just "me and Jesus" with no boundaries (other than those self-imposed), few rules, and very few sacrifices. We are confused by the totality of disciplines, prayers, devotions, and other practices in the Church.

I've heard Archbishop Fulton Sheen say that there are two ways to describe a hospital. The first is to look at the mechanisms within the building. One can describe with callous disregard the magnitude of medical supplies, beds, machines, tubes, doctors, nurses, bureaucracy, sterility, and more. But we can also describe a hospital as a place of caring, healing, curing, safety, nurturing, even of love. It's all in the way we look at it. The Church is a hospital. The Church is there to cure us of the disease of sin, to reunite us with our Father in Heaven, and to help us to enjoy forever the glory of His Kingdom. Every single practice suggested by the Church is meant to serve our eternal salvation.

CULTIVATING THE ART OF SACRIFICE

The saints practiced mortification as a means of obtaining holiness. The following entry from Pope St. John XXIII's journal is a very practical example of how one saint approached mortification:

> As much mortification as possible, especially of the tongue. I must always be ready to humble myself, especially when things go badly. Bodily mortifications are to be few but constant, and without excessive obligation. I will give up salt altogether; I will never eat fruit in the

evening, and never drink more than one glass of wine. As a general rule, I will always leave untouched a mouthful of whatever food is set before me: wine, meat dishes, fruit, pastry, etc. I will never take a morsel of bread over and above the usual amount I find on the table when I begin my meal, nor will I ever mention it to anyone if something is lacking. In general, I will pay more attention to the spirit than to the letter of the mortification, deciding each case on its own merits.[34]

Action

Follow Pope St. John XXIII's example in some small way. Take baby steps and seek God's help in your endeavors:

O blessed Jesus, what I am proposing to do is hard and I feel weak because I am full of self-love, but the will is there and comes from my heart. Help me! Help me![35]

Give up your favorite morning routine one day this week, purely out of love for God.

Do you know that the average American spends roughly $92 per month on coffee?[36] Maybe you could give up that habit for a day or a week. Offer that sacrifice as a gift to God. Say in prayer,

---

[34] Pope John XXIII, *Journal of a Soul* (New York: Image Books, 1980), 95.

[35] Ibid., 119.

[36] Maurie Backman, "Americans Spend More on Coffee Than on Investing," The Motley Fool, January 22, 2018, https://www. fool.com/retirement/2018/01/22/one-third-of-americans-spend-more-on-coffee-than-o.aspx#:~:text=Acorns%20reports%20 that%20the%20average,to%20roughly%20%2492%20a%20 month.

"Lord, I love You more than I love my morning latte." (Note: sacrifice a material routine, such as coffee or breakfast; but do not give up a routine that you already exercise for love of God, such as Mass or spiritual reading.) The grace you receive from that one choice will be monumental. You may not see it. But the spiritual life is not always visible. It is a quiet, humble life that links a soul to God.

If you find the practice of mortification in the spiritual life challenging, keep trying and keep praying for God to strengthen your will. Don't give up, for if you continue to be a slave to the world, you can never truly serve Christ. As He says in Matthew: "No one can serve two masters; for either he will hate the one and love the other, or he will be devoted to the one and despise the other" (Matt. 6:24).

Suggested Reading

An Introduction to the Devout Life, by St. Francis de Sales
To Love Fasting: The Monastic Experience, by Adalbert de Vogüé

7

Beware of Blessings and Curses: The Lie of the Prosperity Gospel

For my thoughts are not your thoughts, neither are
my ways your ways, says the LORD. For as the heavens
are higher than the earth, so are my ways higher than
your ways and my thoughts than your thoughts.

—Isaiah 55:8–9

What do you get when you take a dash of Christianity, stir in about a pound of the American Dream, and marinade them in ten gallons of mouthwatering, high-spirited self-help psychology? You get a recipe for the prosperity gospel, which is being cooked up and served in churches around the world. Even Catholics are falling victim to the dangerous lies being peddled through this philosophy.[37] This lie is a direct result of the modernist heresy: it emphasizes the comforts of this world, claiming that we can expect a utopia here and now.

---

[37] Kate Kingsbury and Andrew Chesnut, "How Catholics Are Falling for the Prosperity Gospel," *Catholic Herald*, November 29, 2018, https://catholicherald.co.uk/magazine/the-liturgy -of-money/.

A belief with roots in Pentecostalism, the prosperity gospel (also known as the health-and-wealth gospel or the gospel of success) preaches that our faith in God is the first step toward winning the jackpot of all jackpots in worldly greatness: vigorous health, euphoric happiness, plenty of money, and a wealth of power and material pleasures in this life. Unlimited dreams are ours for the asking—provided we just have faith.

Proponents of this mouthwatering concoction argue that Christ shed His blood once and for all so that we might not have to sacrifice anymore. Or, as one well-known televangelist said, "Jesus died that we might live an abundant life."[38] According to this notion, Christ's sacrifice was the end of all sacrifice, and His resurrection was the beginning of living in the resurrection. (Could this be why we often see a resurrected Jesus hanging conspicuously in churches where a crucifix once hung?) There are preachers who argue that you and your loved ones need not suffer—if only you have enough faith. Instead, they say, God wills all to be physically healed and financially blessed. Even better, just as your faith will attract all the good things in life, it will repel any misfortunes that fate may have been planning to toss your way.

BIBLICAL FOUNDATIONS

To be honest, even an unschooled preacher could find biblical support for the claim that God blesses those who have faith. Just think about all those blessings doled out in the Old Testament! Beginning with Abraham, God promised him (and his

---

[38] "Pastor Joel Olsteen Responds to Criticism," January 8, 2012, video, 3:36, https://www.youtube.com/watch?v=Qp0-mjxevzs.

descendants) protection, saying that He would bless those who blessed him and curse those who cursed him and that, in him, all families of the earth would be blessed (Gen. 12:3). Through the obedience of faith demonstrated by his father, Abraham, Isaac was also blessed:

> And the LORD appeared to him, and said, "Do not go down to Egypt; dwell in the land of which I shall tell you. Sojourn in this land and I will be with you and will bless you; for to you and to your descendants I will give all these lands, and I will fulfil the oath which I swore to Abraham your father" (Gen. 26:2–3).

God told Isaac that his descendants would be as numerous as "the stars of heaven" (Gen. 26:4).

Even in the New Testament, the prosperity gospel is given some validity. Jesus Himself promises that that He will always provide for those who follow Him: "Therefore do not be anxious, saying, 'What shall we eat?' or 'What shall we drink?' or 'What shall we wear?' For the Gentiles seek all these things; and your heavenly Father knows that you need them all. But seek first his kingdom and his righteousness, and all these things shall be yours as well" (Matt. 6:31–33).[39]

This is awesome! We know beyond a shadow of a doubt that God will take care of us because we have His word on that. But is it possible that our understanding of these verses has been muddled by the culture in which we live? Could it be that the emphasis in our interpretation should be more on the parts that talk about "seeking first his kingdom" or "if we ask

---

[39] See also Deut. 7:9; Ps. 37:4; 2 Cor. 9:8; Rom. 8:32; 1 John 5:14–15.

anything according to his will," as opposed to the parts that suggest getting "whatever we ask"? Maybe it's not His will that I have a new BMW or that my child gets into Harvard. And maybe it's not even His will that my husband be cured of his painful illness. My job is to trust my Heavenly Father — not to gauge His power and goodness on the flawed barometer of my materialism. I must know that whatever happens, it is God's will and is meant for my sanctification and that of those around me. My responsibility is to unite my will with His, not to judge His will according to my checklist of desires, however selfless and virtuous they may be.

AS AMERICAN AS APPLE PIE

While it can be argued that the notion of blessings (and curses) based on one's disposition toward God is corroborated in Sacred Scripture, the extreme nature of "blessing" heralded in the health-and-wealth gospel seems to be a uniquely American tradition (fast making its way around the globe) wherein the treasure of faith and joy found in Christ and rewarded with eternal life in heaven is conflated with all the worldly rewards available in this life.

The prosperity gospel dates back to the late 1800s when a man by the name of E. W. Kenyon began preaching on the power of the mind in securing one's destiny. "Only Christians' rightful use of divine principles could unlock God's treasury of blessings."[40] Kenyon called it "dominating faith."[41] In other words, if we, as

---

[40] Quoted in Kate Bowler, *Blessed: A History of the American Prosperity Gospel* (New York: Oxford University Press, 2013), chap. 1, under "E. W. Kenyon," Kindle ed.

[41] Ibid.

Christians, just believe as we ought and do as we ought, a world of treasures would be placed at our feet. Oral Roberts picked up on this thread and intertwined with it the notion of "seed money" (based on the parable of the mustard seed), a teaching that believers can obtain health and wealth by professing their faith through the sowing of seeds in the form of faithful payments of tithes and offerings. Whatever wording prosperity preachers use, they have always advocated great generosity among their followers. "If you are generous with God, He will surely be generous with you," is a common mantra.

This generosity has made quite the impact. Joel Osteen, undoubtedly the most successful prosperity preacher today, has a net worth $100 million.[42] Lakewood Church — where Osteen presides — is the largest church in America. Clearly, his followers have been generous. Osteen, along with other prosperity preachers, including T. D. Jakes, Creflo Dollar, Joyce Meyer, Kenneth Copeland, and Leroy Thompson, have made the Christian message akin to a self-help or motivational talk that centers on ideas like the power of positive thinking, touted by Rev. Norman Vincent Peale — a pastor himself — who wrote a best-selling book by the same name in 1952.

THE POWER OF POSITIVE THINKING

The idea of faith guaranteeing a life free from pain and suffering is enticing. And Americans are falling for it. According to a poll by *Time*, 61 percent of Christians believe God wants them to be

---

[42] "Joel Osteen Net Worth," Celebrity Net Worth, https://www.celebritynetworth.com/richest-celebrities/joel-osteen-net-worth/.

"prosperous."[43] And some are treating their faith in God like a lottery ticket—just waiting to be cashed in.

George Adams is the perfect example of "prosperity thinking." His story was featured in a *Time* article titled "Does God Want You to Be Rich?" When George lost his factory job in Ohio, he didn't put together a resume or hop on Monster.com. Rather, he uprooted his wife and four kids and relocated to Conroe, Texas, near Lakewood Church, were megapastor Joel Osteen motivates Christians to rise above the fray and claim the riches that God wants for them:

Inspired by the preacher's insistence that one of God's top priorities is to shower blessings on Christians in this lifetime—and by the corollary assumption that one of the worst things a person can do is to expect anything less—Adams marched into Gullo Ford in Conroe looking for work. He didn't have entry-level aspirations: "God has showed me that he doesn't want me to be a run-of-the-mill person," he explains. He demanded to know what the dealership's top salesmen made—and got the job. Banishing all doubt—"You can't sell a $40,000-to-$50,000 car with menial thoughts"—Adams took four days to retail his first vehicle, a Ford F-150 Lariat with leather interior. He knew that many fellow salesmen don't notch their first score until their second week. "Right now, I'm above average!" he exclaims. "It's a new day God has given me! I'm on my way to a six-figure income!"[44]

---

[43] David Van Biema and Jeff Chu, "Does God Want You to Be Rich?" *Time*, September 10, 2006, http://content.time.com/time/magazine/article/0,9171,1533448,00.html.

[44] Ibid.

Before you scoff at the likes of George, ask yourself whether you, too, believe that God will "bless" you in material ways. Is He blessing you when things are going well? And on the flip side, do you think He may be cursing you when they aren't? Do you bargain with God? Or with Mary or some other saint? Do you promise some sort of sacrifice or devotion if only your petition is granted? Or how often do you look at others, thinking they are so "blessed"—blessed with a great family, great job, happy marriage, disposable income, and so forth? It's such a narrow distinction; after all, aren't we supposed to see all gifts from God as "blessings"? The problem lies in linking faith in God to some sort of motivational prescription for worldly success. This results in a temptation to discount divine providence, where God is behind the wheel, and to believe that we are behind the wheel and that God is rewarding our faith, our decisions, in material ways.

I'm not knocking the power of positive thinking or the value inherent in having goals or creating expectations for yourself. There is plenty of research to demonstrate that attitude matters and that goals matter. Certainly, expectations set a tone for our future behavior. But the obvious truth is that God's "blessings" may or may not be directly linked to financial success. After all, some of the most successful people in the world have little faith, while multitudes of saints in history were financially destitute or suffered from debilitating physical or emotional suffering.

Think of the two most notable examples: Jesus and Mary. There are none on earth whose faith could match that of the incarnate God or His holy Mother. And yet neither was ever "rewarded" with riches—at least by earthly standards. Nor has anyone on earth ever endured greater suffering, whether physically or emotionally. If we are thinking that God desires for us great worldly gain as opposed to holiness and perfect union with Him (as Jesus and Mary were so perfectly united), we are seeking "rewards" for something that may be better described as faith in ourselves than faith in God.

This distinction is not a matter of splitting hairs. There is grave danger in peddling something that is so inconsistent with the truth. When Christians are led to believe that their faith will result in a life of health and financial prosperity in this world, they are being led astray. For when believing Christians place all their "trust" in a shell of a faith, it is bound to shatter in the face of tragedy, as it did for two people whom I will call Jason and Melissa Smith.

WHEN POSITIVITY FAILS — A PROFILE

Jason and Melissa Smith belonged to a lively Pentecostal church in the Midwest. They were completely immersed in the Church culture and passionate about their pastor's message, attending services several times a week and centering their lives on God's Word—as far as they understood it. They believed they were meant to lay claim to the gifts Christ promised those who believed that God was big enough to do anything. Melissa says about their mindset at that time, "We were successful and got swept up in being children of 'the King'—and enjoying all the blessings that come with that."

Because they pursued careers and focused on other goals, Jason and Melissa waited longer than most of their friends to begin a family. After twelve years of marriage, they set their hearts on entering that stage of life and felt their faith confirmed and validated when they learned that Melissa was pregnant with identical twins. In the midst of praising God ecstatically for His generosity, the happy couple set about planning for life after doubling their family.

Nothing could have prepared them for what was about to happen.

A sonogram nearly five months into Melissa's pregnancy revealed that one of their babies was suffering from anencephaly, which means that a major portion of her brain and skull were missing. During the devastating meeting, when she was focused on how they were going to solve the problem, Melissa remembers the doctor looking her square in the eye and saying, "You are not understanding. This condition is incompatible with life. When your baby is born, she will die."

Jason and Melissa spent that evening with family, comforting one another and desperately mourning this tragic news, longing to return to the hope and joy they had savored just hours earlier. But as they sat around the kitchen table, discussing their fate, one of Melissa's sisters reminded them of their faith. She said, "Just do that thing you do. Fight. Pray. Believe in Him for her healing."

Prophetically, those words would drive the next two and a half months for Jason and Melissa. They woke the next morning with a new mission — healing. The couple began to read books on faith and healing and sought prayers wherever they could find them. They believed that God would reward their faith and that He willed healing for all. Shortly into their new mission, they learned that Benny Hinn was coming to their metro area. They saw his coming as a sign from God. They needed healing, and Benny Hinn was a world-renowned healer, famous for his "Miracle Crusades." They attended his charismatic tour and left full of hope and excitement. They spent the weeks until Melissa's delivery chasing after God's promises. They told themselves, "If we do all these right things, God will answer our prayers." But as Melissa says now, "I was believing in my ability to believe."

They believed so strongly and so absolutely that when Melissa went into early labor, they were completely unprepared for the turn their lives were about to take. They had never allowed themselves to conceive of the possibility that their precious daughter might actually be born with the devastating illness that had been diagnosed in the womb. Understandably, when little Emily was born, they were in complete shock. Even in the deepest recesses of their hearts and minds, they had fully expected her to be healed. Instead, Jason and Melissa spent ten heart-wrenching days together holding and loving their two little girls before their sweet little Emily passed away in their arms. At that moment, they felt deeply betrayed. Together they vowed to devote the rest of their lives to the love and security of their remaining daughter. But at the same time, they turned their backs on God, whom they felt had cruelly turned His back on them. Their faith had suffered a blow from which it would take years to recover.

GOD HAS A DIFFERENT MESSAGE

Thankfully for Jason and Melissa, their story continued. They learned their lesson the hard way; but in the end, their story became one of conversion when, after running for years, they found Christ in the depths of yet another darkness they could not have foreseen.

After Emily's death, Jason and Melissa did what they could to focus on their only daughter. But rather than suffer from the pain involved in mourning their great loss, they opted to keep themselves busy—turning their attention to opening a new business, following their dream of entrepreneurship. Six months after burying their baby girl, Jason and Melissa entered into a contract to begin building a beautiful, full-service coffee shop in a new suburban shopping center, which they opened the following year.

After spending the next few years focusing every waking hour on business—opening a second coffee shop and also two posh wine bars in upscale urban neighborhoods—2008 happened. With a market crash that caused catastrophic losses from top to bottom in the financial world, traffic for trendy extravagances virtually stopped. Overnight their businesses went from being rated number one in their metro area to being considered lavish "extras" that shell-shocked and cautious consumers could no longer afford. Jason and Melissa found themselves overextended, and their financial world began to crumble. In the fiscal fallout, they felt they had been shoved into the pit of Hell, being sued by once happy investors, accused of embezzlement, with IRS liens and bankruptcy staring them in the face. They had reporters at their doorstep, investigators calling at all hours, unpaid bills piling up, and the only home their daughter had known being foreclosed upon. Jason and Melissa had hit rock bottom.

Melissa describes their experience this way:

> We went off and pursued our worldly dreams without God. We didn't go to church and didn't even talk to God for many years. We still believed in Him, but we were no longer followers. We did not live our lives for Him. When the business tumbled around us, it was a very dark place. I will never forget the night that we came back to God. There was so much fear and oppression. We had a lawsuit, bankruptcy, reporters accusing us of embezzling, etc.

Everything was caving in on us, and we could even feel a demonic presence in our house. And then one night, at two or three in the morning, unable to sleep because of the strain, [Jason] was crying, and I was beside myself with helplessness. I looked at him and said very simply and quietly, "What about God?" And then together we began to pray.

Instantly there was peace.

After that moment of recognition, of conversion, nothing changed in their outward situation. Jason and Melissa lost everything. They lost their businesses, their house, and all their retirement savings. They owed $250,000 to the IRS and endured being sued by former friends and business associates. Perhaps most painful were the strained relationships with family members who had lost retirement savings after investing in their business. But Jason and Melissa knew that God was with them through it all, and they felt peace for the first time in years. They remained happy through all the fallout; Melissa says, "As it turns out, He was actually all we really needed."

Looking back, Melissa says that when they went through their first tragedy, they never sought "the Healer." They sought only His healing. Instead of loving God for who He was, they saw God as a gift bearer. The second time around, they clung to Christ in the midst of the chaos. This time, they had their eyes on the Healer Himself, for who He was and not for what He could do for them. He didn't take their suffering away, but He was right there with them through it all. Melissa says that she and Jason realized that true happiness is not about having God give us what we want. True joy comes from having a relationship with Him and being transformed in the process.

A WORLD AWAY FROM TRUTH

The idea that Christ died for us and therefore we are meant to live on easy street would not make sense to 90 percent of the Christian population in the world who suffer from devastating economic circumstances and tragic health conditions. Despite their trials and sufferings, these members of the Christian faithful live joy-filled lives of gratitude and peace.

One thing we find, all too often, is that even when we try to avoid pain, it seems to find its way to us. We cannot possibly control every aspect of life. It doesn't matter how many balls we try to juggle just so. In the end, we realize that we are not in control. But we can use the inevitability of pain to our advantage. We can use it to grow in holiness, to learn to submit our wills to the will of Almighty God, for it is only in carrying the cross that we can truly unite our hearts to the Heart of our Savior.

Sometimes success in this world can thwart the intimate relationship that Christ seeks with each of us. We begin to rely on ourselves, and we build an expectation around our ability to control our lives. We have little need for God when we believe we can take care of ourselves. Years later, Melissa explained that before her pregnancy, she and Jason felt as if they were in complete control:

> If I wanted to drive to work or go out to eat, or build my business or pursue a lavish lifestyle, I believed I just made a decision and presto — it became real. Not until we suffered Emily's illness and death did we realize that really, it is only by God's grace that I can go to work or build my business. Very easily I could get into a tragic accident or suffer a monumental failure in our business because the market takes a dive — really we are not in control at all.

The truth is that God is in control, and we are at the mercy of His providence. To the extent that we unite ourselves to Him, that union can grow stronger, even in the face of tragedy. In fact, Jason and Melissa believe that God used both of the most painful periods in their lives to draw them closer to Him. Through a long and arduous journey, Jason and Melissa have recognized their great need for God and for His providence.

The health-and-wealth gospel is dangerous because it fools us into believing that somehow we are the arbiters of our own destiny. If we only believe enough, give generously enough, live well enough, then we will be materially and spiritually "blessed." This implies that my well-being is a matter of my own desire. If I can name it, I can claim it. Jason and Melissa learned that this is not the case. Sometimes those things we cannot control allow us the opportunity to grow in ways that we may not have imagined for ourselves.

CULTIVATING THE ART OF SACRIFICE

It's difficult to walk that line between living in this world and not being of this world. I often find myself asking God how He can allow us to be up to our eyeballs in a materialistic world and not expect us to become materialistic? It's so difficult to surround ourselves with the beauty and truth of God when the world is so *loud*. It's like asking ourselves to focus on the song of a nightingale while we're standing in the middle of a war zone.

It's a difficult battle. But God has promised us that He is the only ammunition we need. He will provide the grace necessary for us to hear the song. Let God's Word be our inspiration as we stare down the lies of the health-and-wealth gospel.

"Set your mind on things that are above, not on things that are on earth" (Col. 3:2).

Action

We have messages about worldly goodness coming at us twenty-four hours a day. Fight fire with fire. Schedule fifteen to thirty minutes today (the sooner, the better) for spiritual reading. Read Sacred Scripture, spiritual classics, or the *Catechism*. Whatever you do, spend that time in a spirit of prayer so that you might be better prepared for those spiritual battles you encounter every day in the world.

Make the small sacrifice of spiritual reading a daily commitment, and stick to it. If you can do only fifteen minutes now, gradually work your way up to at least thirty by adding five minutes to your daily schedule each week. You'll be amazed at the wisdom you will be able to carry with you throughout the day—wisdom that will profoundly deepen your interior life and strengthen your resolve.

Suggested Reading

The Imitation of Christ, by Thomas à Kempis
Transformation in Christ, by Dietrich von Hildebrand

8

Beware of Wolves in Sheep's Clothing: The Lie of Socialism

You are aware indeed, that the goal of this most iniquitous plot is to drive people to overthrow the entire order of human affairs and to draw them over to the wicked theories of this Socialism and Communism, by confusing them with perverted teachings.

—Pope Pius IX, *Nostis et Nobiscum* 6

My kids were raised listening to Dave Ramsey, a well-known radio personality who shuns debt and promotes wise financial decisions. As a result, our first three have been attending college without any debt. And any and all costs for college have come out of their own pockets—not from Dad and Mom. For our oldest, that has meant attending a state school in lieu of a more expensive, private school. It has also meant working more than eighty hours per week through the summers and full-time during the school year in addition to his studies in order to pay room, board, and tuition out of pocket. He made the choice to sacrifice materially in many ways, so that he might avoid debt and prepare himself for a solid future. Over the past three years, he has foregone social functions, internships, vacations, and much more, while watching his friends enjoy the benefits of all three.

Those sacrifices were his choice, and when he graduates, he will look back and feel grateful and proud of his accomplishment.

But as he embarks on his professional career, saving for a home and reaping the rewards of his hard work while others spend their first years repaying what they borrowed, what do you suppose will happen if suddenly, student loans are "forgiven"? Do you think such a turn of events will engender goodwill and love of neighbor from my son? Will it help him to open his heart toward others and to grow in generosity? Or is there a great risk that he will become bitter as he watches his hard-earned income go toward paying for the college loans of others who did not sacrifice as he did? Well, I can answer that question for you because he has already told me. He would be bitter. He has noted that there would be a huge difference between his using his hard-earned "wealth" to give from his heart to someone who is struggling and having his hard-earned income taken from him to pay off loans for someone else — loans that he worked so hard to avoid.

So is my son cruel? Heartless? Selfish? No. I would posit that he's human. And in his situation, many of us would feel the same. This is something the Church has understood for centuries.

SOCIALISM UNDERMINES OUR DESIRE TO LOVE

There is a lie being touted in the public square that has been steadily gaining ground in recent years. That lie is socialism. Socialists proclaim compassion, promise to answer domestic problems with financial commitments, and appeal to a Catholic desire to love our neighbor by pledging to "lift up the poor and the marginalized" and by promoting "social justice" and the "common good." These ideas have been promoted by the Church since her inception.

Unfortunately, with regard to sacrifice, socialism may be the most deceptive lie around. This lie creeps up on Christians, feeding on our compassionate nature, our ordained call to serve, to love our neighbor, and to ensure that justice is served among those most in need. But in fact, to the extent that socialist policies are brought to bear, they will undermine our compassion, inhibit our service, remove the natural relationship we have with our neighbor and destroy the very outcome of justice it professes to serve. As one can foresee in my son's situation, socialism undermines our desire to love.

SOUL-TO-SOUL CONTACT

Given the chance, throughout history Americans have done an amazing job of serving the poor, in both body and soul. But the beautiful thing about the personal connection between two parties is that assistance can be provided and received both with a gracious hand and a discerning eye. Close proximity allows each to evaluate the fruits of cooperation with Gods' grace—whether one's generosity is helping to lift a man from the depths or enabling him to wallow in misery by his own choice. In other words, if I offer someone food or a job or a place to stay, just through my close proximity and relationship with him, I can discern whether my assistance is helpful or whether it is enabling poor habits or decisions.

When it comes to works of mercy, the Catholic Church has been at the forefront of the action. By no means has the Church ever abandoned the poor but she has extended in love the beautiful gifts offered by the Body of Christ. She knows that while God has commissioned His people with the Two Great Commandments, He has also given them free will. And in order for one to love truly, his gift must be offered freely.

There is great danger both to the souls of those in need and to the souls of those with means, should an outside force step in and demand that all men be made to "enjoy" equal outcomes. The Church has been shouting this from the rooftops; but somewhere along the line, our obligation to the poor has been reduced to an economic obligation, and the souls of the needy have been forgotten. Likewise with the giver. His gift has been reduced to a mere economic transaction. There is no relationship between the two. Their eyes do not meet; their souls do not connect. As a result, each suffers greatly.

In God's design, the relationship between the poor and any benefactor is not really one between giver and receiver but one between *giver* and *giver*, *receiver* and *receiver*. For the two benefit equally when sacrifice is offered in love. Sadly, this material-driven world has demeaned man — both rich and poor — by reducing him to a mere material being. Headlines and taglines and hapless phrases have caused us to forget the notion of our fallen nature, of the soul, of our need for affiliation, bonding, freedom — our need to be touched by the hand of God through His Body, the Church.

Many unsuspecting Catholics have bought into socialist promises without recognizing the lies. The intentions of those embracing socialism and voting for its proponents and policies may be well-placed. But socialism is dangerous because it placates our desire to do good without our actually having to *do* good. It rallies around Catholic principles of human dignity and social justice while sticking a dagger into the hearts of both. It uses Christian terms and advocates Christian principles while undermining Christianity. Goodness and love must be chosen. They must be an intricate piece of our participation in the Body of Christ.

As a body, we are one, living, breathing, natural organism in mind, heart, and soul. We are profoundly connected to one another in solidarity, such that the need of one man is the need of all. The sin of one man is the sin of all. On the flip side, the love of one man is the love of all. Our role is to receive the grace offered by the Holy Spirit through the sacraments and, by extension, through prayers, sacraments, and devotions and to go out into the world and spread that grace through love of neighbor.

Socialism cuts that love off at the pass by *compelling* us to give not to our neighbor but to a faceless, unfeeling, uncaring bureaucracy; and then for our gift to be distributed to the poor, again not by a neighbor, but by a faceless, unfeeling, uncaring bureaucracy. To implement socialism is to destroy the living, breathing heart and soul of the Body of Christ and replace it with a cold, mechanical, unbeating prosthesis.

Archbishop Fulton Sheen shares some wise insight that you may find interesting. He said that pre-communist Russians were prophetic, believing that

> the Antichrist would "come disguised as the Great Humanitarian; he will talk peace, prosperity and plenty not as means to lead us to God, but as ends in themselves.... He will be so broad-minded as to identify tolerance with indifference to right and wrong, truth and error; he will spread the lie that men will never be better until they make society better and thus have selfishness to provide fuel for the next revolution.... He will increase love for love and decrease love for person.[45]

---

[45] Fulton J. Sheen, *Communism and the Conscience of the West* (New Pekin, IN: Refuge of Sinners Publishing, 1948), 24.

THE LOST ART OF SACRIFICE

There is grave danger in promoting issues rather than personal relationships. This has become evident in our world as we witness the violent anger begin shown toward individuals in the name of a group or a cause.

THE CROSS WITHOUT CHRIST

Several years ago I read a book called *Nothing to Envy: Ordinary Lives in North Korea*. Written by a journalist who captured in minute detail the day-to-day lives of six North Korean citizens who eventually escaped to freedom in South Korea, the book illustrates the horrid conditions of many in a country that strains to present itself as a utopian society. Ordinary citizens watched loved ones tortured and killed. They ate rats in order to stay alive. Daily lives were nightmares from which citizens could find no escape. Oppressed and desperate, each of these individuals risked life and limb just to get out from under the incredible burden of communism (technically, *socialism*).

The most disturbing and discomforting part of this book was the sacrifice lauded by the government. The talk from their leaders sounded startlingly familiar. These are the themes I hear during Mass every Sunday and read in Sacred Scripture every day. They were the profound ideals offered by the saints who have gone before us. Here's one example of the themes saturating North Korean culture through the hand of their *omnipotent* leader:

> Every town in North Korea, no matter how small, has a movie theater, thanks to Kim Jong-il's conviction that film is an indispensable tool for instilling loyalty in the masses.... The films were mostly dramas with the same themes: The path to happiness was self-sacrifice

and suppression of the individual for the good of the collective.[46]

Sacrifice? Suppression of *self*? These are things I had read for years in the great classics of our Faith. This is what we teach our children. And yet, these sentiments came from an evil, communist dictator. Here evil had coopted the language and the practice of the good. The devil is nothing if not cunning and manipulative. Regardless, when I finished *Nothing to Envy*, I was perplexed, confused. I kept asking myself how something so good and something so terribly evil could sound so similar? What was I missing?

Enter *Life of Christ*, by Archbishop Fulton Sheen. In the first couple of pages, Sheen addresses this very subject. In a few sentences he brought clarity to my confusion:

> Communism has chosen the Cross in the sense that it has brought back to an egotistic world a sense of discipline, self-abnegation, surrender, hard work, study, and dedication to supra-individual goals. But the Cross without Christ is sacrifice without love. Hence, Communism has produced a society that is authoritarian, cruel, oppressive of human freedom, filled with concentration camps, firing squads, and brain-washings.[47]

Socialism is a lie that seeks to separate us from Christ. As in North Korea, socialists promote sacrifice for the common good, to the detriment of human dignity. Whether they recognize their

---

[46] Barbara Demick, *Nothing to Envy: Ordinary Lives in North Korea* (New York: Spiegel & Grau Trade Paperbacks, 2015), 14–15.

[47] Fulton J. Sheen, *Life of Christ* (New York: Image Books, 2008), xxv.

errors or not is a moot point. It turns out that socialists have long preyed on the goodwill of Christians in order to manipulate them into helping achieve socialism's evil ends. In *The Communist Manifesto*, Marx says,

> Has not Christianity declaimed against private property, against marriage, against the state? Has it not preached in the place of these, charity and poverty, celibacy, and mortification of the flesh, monastic life and Mother Church? Christian socialism is but the holy water with which the priest consecrates the heart-burnings of the aristocrat.[48]

Those who promote socialism use our Christian call to manipulate us into subverting our precious freedom—a freedom that allows us, with our families, to see and choose God. According to the *Catechism*,

> God created man a rational being, conferring on him the dignity of a person who can initiate and control his own actions. "God willed that man should be 'left in the hand of his own counsel,' so that he might of his own accord seek his Creator and freely attain his full and blessed perfection by cleaving to him (GS 17; Sir 15:14)." (1730)

Cleaving to God is the path whereby we can obtain the grace that allows us to love enough to sacrifice our own wants, our own needs, our own desires for the good of another.

There is no love without sacrifice. But in a political system, sacrifice without love becomes a distorted perversion of the sacred, used by the few to control the many. No version of this is

---

[48] Karl Marx and Friedrich Engels, *The Communist Manifesto* (Arlington Heights, IL: Harlan Davidson, 1955), 35.

the solution to our nation's problems. True love offered as true sacrifice is the only real solution to what ails us. And it cannot be found in any law, mandate, or government system. In fact, some systems — socialism in particular — can serve as a deterrent to loving sacrifice, the only sacrifice that unites itself to the Cross.

CULTIVATING THE ART OF SACRIFICE

Socialists preach sacrifice for your fellow man. But the entire rationalization for their existence rests on the presumption that man will not "love" his neighbor without some outside influence forcing his hand. They believe that people have given their allegiance to the almighty dollar at the expense of those around them. If someone were to observe you on any given day, would you give them reason to believe otherwise? Ask God to infuse you with a love of neighbor that extends beyond the material, to forge a union that extends from heart to heart, and soul to soul.

Action

1. The Church has always stood in solidarity with men and against socialism. This week, look into ways that you can help the Church fulfill her mission — whether it's donating an extra portion of your paycheck to a particular ministry of Catholic Charities, or looking into what it takes to volunteer to teach the Faith to children and teens in your parish — something sorely needed today. Whatever it is, find a mission in the Church that you'd like to serve with your time, talent, or treasure, and follow through.

2. Knowing the great spiritual battles facing the Church and the world in his time, Pope Leo XIII composed the prayer to St. Michael the Archangel. There are various accounts regarding what inspired him to write it when he did; regardless of the immediate inspiration, he knew that we needed a supernatural warrior to help battle the great demons of socialism and communism. We most certainly need that warrior today. If you don't already do so, make it a practice to say the St. Michael prayer daily:

> St. Michael the Archangel,
> defend us in battle.
> Be our defense against the wickedness
> and snares of the Devil.
> May God rebuke him, we humbly pray,
> and do thou,
> O Prince of the heavenly hosts,
> by the power of God,
> thrust into hell Satan,
> and all the evil spirits,
> who prowl about the world
> seeking the ruin of souls. Amen.

Suggested Reading

Quod Apostolici Muneris by Pope Leo XIII
Rerum Novarum by Pope Leo XIII

9

Beware the Gospel of Death:
Lies about Suffering

*Suffering, pain — failure — is but a kiss of Jesus,
a sign that you have come so close to Jesus on the Cross
that He can kiss you. — So my child be happy. . . .
Do not be discouraged . . . smile back. . . .
For you it is a most beautiful chance of
becoming fully & totally all for Jesus.*

—Saint Teresa of Calcutta[49]

How can a "good" God allow such horrendous suffering and diabolical evil in the world? This is a question that perplexes even the most accepting of souls as we turn on the news and are accosted with horrific stories that test the bounds of our imaginations. Our concerns are magnified when we witness the suffering of our loved ones, borne through no fault of their own, or when we ourselves experience physical, spiritual, or relational pain that we cannot explain.

Common answers to this most important of questions can range from "We just don't know," to "This is God's way of punishing us,"

---

[49] Mother Teresa, *Come Be My Light*, 282.

neither of which is even remotely satisfactory. The first answer is an affront to our need to know and to understand and to make sense of the world around us. The second projects a cruel and heartless God filled with vengeance and bent on retribution. This image just doesn't square with a God of love.

Suffering is a challenging subject because so much suffering is unfathomable and yet seems absolutely pointless, and even cruel. What are we to make of this senseless evil? A common explanation for suffering is that "Bad things happen to good people because of sin." According to one pastor, "Sin brings death, disease, sorrow, loss and suffering.... That's what sin does." This is true. God has blessed us with the gift of free will: we have the power to unite our wills with His (which is what He most desires for us) and the power to thwart His will through the sinful pursuit of our passions and desires.

Unfortunately, if we leave the explanation there—that God allows us to make our own choices and that the free choice to sin will tragically affect the world around us—we make God out to be sort of helpless in the face of sin and death. We go through life thinking that God is not really in control of everything. If sin is the cause of pain and God is hands-off in that department, then, sure, He may have tried His best to protect us; but our first parents pretty much did us in. We begin to believe that because of sin, we are vulnerable to all kinds of horrible suffering. Understandably, this leaves us fearful, worrying from moment to moment that if we are not careful, sin and death may find us and there's nothing God can do about it.

And yet, Christ, in His Sermon on the Mount, warns His disciples against all this worrying: "And which of you by being anxious can add one cubit to his span of life?" (Matt. 6:27).

HE'S GOT THE WHOLE WORLD IN HIS HANDS

God knows that worrying serves no purpose. Instead, He wants us to trust Him with our entire being, even in our suffering, or through the suffering of those we love. And we can do that, because we know that God is in control of all things.

You see, although God is not the author of sin, He is the author of everything else. And everything that happens (even sin) is under His control, guided lovingly through His divine providence. For, though God does not cause sin to happen, He does indeed govern it, because God's will governs all things. In other words, God controls everything, both good and bad, through His holy will.[50]

Look no further than Sacred Scripture for confirmation:

The LORD kills and brings to life; he brings down to Sheol and raises up. The LORD makes poor and makes rich; he brings low, he also exalts. (1 Sam. 2:6–7)

Good things and bad, life and death, poverty and wealth, come from the Lord. (Sir. 11:14)

The LORD gave, and the LORD has taken away; blessed be the name of the LORD. (Job 1:21)

But how can this be, we ask? God is all good; so how can He cause bad things to happen to us?

Often we think of God only in terms of His active will. For us, this means that God can cure cancer or save us from harm. While His active will certainly moves as a current through the world,

---

[50] Father Jean Baptiste Saint-Jure, S.J., and Saint Claude de la Colombière, *Trustful Surrender to Divine Providence: The Secret of Peace and Happiness* (Charlotte, NC: TAN Books, 1980), 10.

we must remember that God also has what is called a passive will. This is the will that allows things to happen. For example, I may wonder how it is that my father-in-law was forced to endure such suffering, eventually dying a painful death from bone cancer, while my friend was released from its clutches with very little suffering at all. The truth is that God allowed that cancer to remain with my father-in-law when He very well could have cured it. Think about it. If we believe that God can heal someone, mustn't we also believe that sometimes He chooses *not* to heal (at least in a physical sense)?

Do we know why? Perhaps not, but we should trust that God causes or allows all things for our benefit. This is a key component to the "We don't know why bad things happen" explanation for suffering. We may not know. But we don't need to know; because we know that God knows, and that He is ultimately in control.

God does want us to know that everything He allows to happen to us will help us grow in holiness, will sanctify us, and—most importantly—will serve to unite us to Him, so long as we trust Him and cooperate with His grace.

Again, we must remember that we are not on this earth for earthly glory; rather, this life is but the means to our true home, which is heaven. For each one of us, God has chosen the perfect path—one that best leads us to Him. No matter the suffering, great or small, physical or spiritual, the result of natural disaster or evil intention, God allows it for good reason, and we can rest comfortably knowing that He indeed has the whole world in His hands, holding us gently, loving us completely, guiding us to perfect union with Him.

GOD DESIRES ONLY OUR GOOD

God desires eternal union with each one of us, which He also makes clear in Scripture:

The glory which thou hast given me I have given to them, that they may be one even as we are one, I in them and thou in me, that they may become perfectly one, so that the world may know that thou hast sent me and hast loved them even as thou hast loved me. (John 17:22–23)

In light of this, one of the most beautiful teachings of the Catholic Church is that suffering has meaning and purpose. We can say this because when we suffer, we know that God has allowed our suffering only because He truly loves us and desires what is best for us, like a parent who opts not to give a child the desires of her heart because he knows much better than the child what will lead her to true happiness. Sometimes the discipline of a parent is painful for a child. But then growing in virtue and responsibility is often challenging and may even be very painful in the short-term.

But what about indescribable suffering? What about horrible atrocities committed against innocent victims, which change people's lives forever? Even here, we can be comforted in knowing that all suffering is a gift from God and that He allows such pain only for the betterment of our souls and for the benefit of His Body, the Church. In *Trustful Surrender to Divine Providence*, Father Jean Baptiste Saint-Jure shares St. Gregory's analogy of a doctor, offered at a time when doctors commonly used leeches to purify a patient's blood by drawing out disease:

A doctor, he says, orders leeches to be applied. While these small creatures are drawing blood from the patient their only aim is to gorge themselves and suck up as much of it as they can. The doctor's only intention is to have the impure blood drawn from the patient and to cure him in this manner. There is, therefore no relation between the insatiable greed of the leeches and the intelligent purpose of the doctor in using them. The patient himself does not protest their use. He does not regard the leeches as evildoers. Rather he tries to overcome the repugnance the sight of their ugliness causes and help them in their action, in the knowledge that the doctor has judged it useful for his health.

God makes use of men as the doctor does of leeches. Neither should we then stop to consider the evilness of those to whom God gives power to act on us or to be grieved at their wicked intentions, and we should keep ourselves from feelings of aversion towards them.[51]

No matter the sorrow, no matter the pain, we can be sure that God has administered a sweet salve to heal us of all our wounds, to purify us, that we might be prepared to experience the eternal joy that He has in store for us.

Count it all joy, my brethren, when you meet various trials, for you know that the testing of your faith produces steadfastness. And let steadfastness have its full effect, that you may be perfect and complete, lacking in nothing.... Blessed is the man who endures trial, for when he has stood the test he will receive the crown of life which God has promised to those who love him. (James 1:2–4, 12)

So, as you wonder how you might make it through this time of suffering—as you ask the all-encompassing question of the suffering around the globe, that simple but profound, "Why me?" —know that your sufferings and the sufferings of those you love

---

[51] Saint-Jure and de la Colombière, *Trustful Surrender*, 15–16.

serve a great purpose. You may not know that purpose at the moment, but trust that your Father in Heaven has granted a loving gift that will serve both your body and soul.

YOU WERE THERE ALL ALONG

Several years ago, my children and I read C. S. Lewis's *The Horse and His Boy*, the third book in Lewis's Narnia series. The day after we relished the final words and replaced the book upon the shelf, Hurricane Katrina tore its way through New Orleans and destroyed the gulf coast from Central Florida to Texas. In the coming days, like the rest of the country, my husband and I were riveted to the news. My oldest was only six, but he was observant and asked a simple version of the same question that was being asked by thousands of others at the time: How could God allow something like this to happen?

It's possible that *The Horse and His Boy* became my favorite Narnia book specifically because of Hurricane Katrina. The story helped me to answer a profound question in simple terms that our kids could understand. The main character, Shasta, as well as his companion, Aravis, and their horses, Bree and Hwin, endure many hardships throughout their adventures together. At one point, Shasta is terribly hungry and is walking alone through the pitch-black night, feeling sorry for himself in the midst of all his misfortunes, when he senses a large creature walking alongside him. Mentally, he tries to strategize how he is going to save himself, but no matter how hard he thinks about it, he cannot figure out how to get away. Finally, he can stand the deafening silence between himself and the creature no longer, so he begins to speak and is shocked by the exchange. Once he is assured that the creature will not harm him, Shasta uses the opportunity for companionship to complain about all that has happened to him and how terribly unlucky he has been:

> He told how he had never known his real father or mother and had been brought up sternly by the fisherman. And then he told the story of his escape and how they were chased by lions and forced to swim for their lives; and of all their dangers in Tashbaan and about his night among the tombs and how the beasts howled at him out of the desert. And he told about the heat and thirst of their desert journey and how they were almost at their goal when another lion chased them and wounded Aravis. And also, how very long it was since he had had anything to eat.

The creature begs to differ, assuring Shasta that he has not been unfortunate at all. Shasta argues that surely, at the very least, encountering so many lions must have been unlucky? The creature's answer should serve as a lesson for the rest of us:

> "I was the lion." And as Shasta gaped with open mouth and said nothing, the Voice continued. "I was the lion who forced you to join with Aravis. I was the cat who comforted you among the houses of the dead. I was the lion who drove the jackals from you while you slept. I was the lion who gave the horses the new strength of fear for the last mile so that you should reach King Lune in time. And I was the lion you do not remember who pushed the boat in which you lay, a child near death, so that it came to the shore where a man sat, wakeful at midnight, to receive you."[52]

---

[52] C. S. Lewis, *The Horse and His Boy* (New York: HarperTrophy, 2000), 161–166.

Throughout the book, adventures that had appeared as grave misfortunes worked together to serve their ultimate purpose, to reunite Shasta with his father, King Lune, and his long-lost twin brother and to bring Shasta to his rightful position as heir to the throne in Archenland.

When bad things happen, with great exasperation, we look up, shake our fists and ask "Why?" Why did tornadoes destroy so many homes and lives in Oklahoma? Why the bombing at the Boston Marathon? Why did my father (or mother or sister or friend or child) have to die of cancer? Why was that child abused by the people who were supposed to love him most? Why did my husband lose his job? Why? Why? Why?

But don't we share Shasta's ultimate purpose — to be re-united with our Father and Brother and to inherit the Kingdom of Heaven? Shasta's story beautifully illustrates how our misfortunes, too, can work together for our greater good, leading us out of exile and back to our Father's home, where we belong.

St. Paul tells us that we are "heirs of God and fellow heirs with Christ, provided we suffer with him in order that we may also be glorified with him" (Rom. 8:17). If this is true — and it is — then, rather than wallowing in our sufferings, we should follow St. Paul's example and rejoice in them (Rom. 5:3; Col. 1:24).

The fact is, we may not understand why bad things happen. But in the midst of every tragedy, as we pick up the pieces and help those around us, we should remember that there is a big picture. We just can't quite see it yet.

As Father (now Bishop) Robert Baron explains in his book *The Strangest Way,* "We are like a person surveying Georges Seurat's pointillist masterpiece *Sunday Afternoon on la Grand Jatte* with his nose pressed against the canvas. That picture reveals its meaning only as one steps back from it, and the colors begin to blend and the lights and darks gradually arrange themselves into patterns. What we see of God the Artist's work are bits and pieces of His studio or one tiny corner of His endlessly complex pointillist canvas."[53]

But one day, we will back up and see the painting as it was meant to be seen—at a distance, in all its grand majesty.

And at that moment, by God's grace, we'll be able to say, "So that was You all the time!"[54] For now, when those moments that we do not understand come, we must bow our heads and pray, "Jesus, I trust in You."

WE CAN PARTICIPATE IN THE REDEMPTION

But there is more to the story. Not only do we know that God has ordained each and every moment of our lives to draw us down a path that will unite us to our Heavenly Father; in addition, God, in His divine mercy, invites us to unite our suffering to His sacrifice on the Cross. In fact, it is His Cross that gives our suffering meaning, as we saw with Elisabeth Leseur. As part of His Mystical Body, we can offer our pain and sorrow alongside Christ's pain and sorrow. His Cross has the power to turn what can often be wretchedly ugly suffering into a beautiful sacrifice of redemption and grace. According to Archbishop Fulton Sheen in his book *The Mystical Body of Christ*,

> Our sorrows, and tears, our mortifications and our promises have no intrinsic merit in themselves.... Suppose

---

[53] Robert Barron, *The Strangest Way: Walking the Christian Path* (Maryknoll, NY: Orbis Books, 2002), 141.

[54] C. S. Lewis, *The Screwtape Letters* (San Francisco: HarperSanFrancisco, 2000), 174.

now we unite them with our Lord so that they are made part of the infinite merit of Calvary; suppose we offer them to our Lord so that they are His, and His name is stamped on them, then they become precious because they are part of the very sacrifice of Christ; only when they are crucified with Christ do they hold the pledge of an everlasting Easter.[55]

This is not about achieving salvation as an accomplishment. Offering our suffering to God is about participating with God in the very act of salvation. Not only our physical suffering, but our spiritual suffering also can also produce great fruit. For most of us, long-suffering in the wake of small inconveniences and frustrations is one of the most available gifts to give, but perhaps also the most difficult. To offer those everyday challenges might be even more laudable than acts of great heroism admired in the public square. Think about how much more difficult it would be to give of ourselves in kindness and patience, day in and day out, regardless of the annoyances and petty issues involving our family, friends or co-workers, than to jump in front of a bullet in effort to save a life. The latter is a momentary decision, most likely causing momentary pain, followed by an eternity of joy. The former requires a lifetime of exercising the fruits of the Holy Spirit. We must spend each moment calling upon the Holy Spirit to help us practice the virtues of love, joy, peace, patience, kindness, goodness, gentleness, faithfulness, and self-control (see Gal. 5:22–23). But in the process, our loving gifts may help save more souls than taking a bullet ever could.

Fr. Walter Ciszek, who endured twenty-three years in Soviet prisons and labor camps after having been declared a "Vatican

---

[55] Sheen, *Mystical Body*, 244.

Spy" during World War II, beautifully demonstrated the power of suffering:

> No matter how harsh the conditions in the camps might be, how cruel and useless the work might seem, it took on new meaning and added value. It was something of which a man could be proud each day, because it was his to offer back to God. Each day of labor and hardship, like the grains of wheat ground up to make the host at Mass, could be consecrated to God and be transformed into something of great value in God's sight; it was a sacrifice each man could offer back to God throughout the long, hard days. The grinding routine of daily labor, even here in Siberia, could have a meaning, did have a value, even as the lives of all men everywhere—no matter how dull or routine or insignificant they might seem to the eyes of men—have value and a meaning in God's providence.[56]

Ciszek did not suffer passively. He offered his afflictions back to God as a gift. What is the difference? When we accept suffering as something that must be endured, we become mere victims. On the other hand, when we choose to accept God's will lovingly, to trust Him with everything we are and everything we have—to offer each moment back to Him for our sanctification, or for the sanctification of others—this is sacrifice. This is love. This is when we participate in the redemption of the world. And *this* is when suffering becomes powerful.

So today, embrace God's will for all those moments you can't control. Whether mere inconveniences or the great chalice of

---

[56] Fr. Walter Ciszek, *He Leadeth Me* (San Francisco: Ignatius Press, 1995), 141–142.

suffering, offer them up as a loving gift to God. Don't just accept your trials, floating down the river of life wherever the current takes you. Don't shuffle along like Eeyore, with a fatalistic, if submissive attitude, as in "Well, I guess if this is God's will, I'll just plod along, feeling sorry for myself." Rather, today is a new day! So participate in God's will by offering your suffering (great or small) as a sacrifice of love!

Carry your cross so that it will be, as St. Josemaría Escrivá calls it, a "Holy Cross." He says that when you love the cross, it becomes "a Cross, without a Cross."[57]

WHAT DOES REDEMPTIVE SUFFERING DO FOR ME?

Just as perfect contrition is always most desirable, a perfect gift of love is the more preferable and meritorious. Nonetheless, considering the benefits that abound when we offer our suffering for the salvation of souls might just validate for us the awesome paradox of our Faith:

1. Hope. Regardless of how painful, how permanent, how hopeless our suffering can seem in its own right, redemptive suffering turns all that sadness into joy, in that we can know it is not needless or senseless. Instead, our suffering can have tremendous purpose.

2. At a time when we are most tempted to turn inward, to wrap ourselves in pity for our wretched state, to feed off our pain, becoming self-absorbed and sullen, redemptive suffering offers us an opportunity to turn

---

[57] St. Josemaría Escrivá, *The Holy Rosary* (New York: Scepter, 2003), Fourth Sorrowful Mystery.

toward others; toward our Heavenly Father, toward our neighbor. It offers an opportunity to give.

3. In suffering, there are times when we can do nothing for ourselves. We must humbly accept the service of others in even the most basic matters of our lives. But redemptive suffering allows us to do something even when we can seemingly do nothing. Offering our suffering to God for the salvation of souls or for some other special intention gives us an opportunity to serve others even in the face of physical or emotional barriers that would seem to inhibit our ability to give.

4. It is an answer to all those who say that suffering should be avoided at all costs. On the contrary, suffering may bring about the most good in the natural world, when it is offered in love for the salvation of souls.

Through St. Faustina, Christ promises that our sacrificial union with Him will produce much fruit:

> You will save more souls through prayer and suffering than will a missionary through his teachings and sermons alone.[58]

Of course, I am not suggesting that you cause unnecessary suffering or that you seek out pain for this purpose. We all know through experience that providence offers innumerable opportunities to offer our sufferings without our creating them of our own accord. But keep in mind the amazing gift we've

---

[58] *Diary of Saint Maria Faustina Kowalska: Divine Mercy in My Soul* (Stockbridge, MA: Marian Press, 2012), 627, entry 1767.

been given in redemptive suffering when you next have the opportunity to unite your cross with Christ's. Through the grace of God, your sacrifices may just merit the salvation of those souls in most need of His mercy — particularly that soul who concerns you most.

CULTIVATING THE ART OF SACRIFICE

Whatever the cause or level of pain, suffering can be a lonely condition. No matter how much our loved ones try to understand, they cannot see into the depths of our souls to know the extent of our true agony. Perhaps you could you use your suffering as an opportunity to draw closer to our Heavenly Father, who comforts us in all our afflictions (1 Cor. 1:4). It's not that we shouldn't confide in friends or loved ones. But at some point, try pouring out your heart to God, who alone can give you rest.

Action

1. If you are suffering through anything right now, tell yourself that you may have no control over the pain but that misery is a choice. Don't let pain — whether yours or a loved one's — make you bitter and resentful. Instead, offer a prayer of gratitude for the opportunity to become more Christlike, and offer your suffering up to Christ for the salvation of sinners, both those in your home and those in the world.

2. Pray a Divine Mercy Chaplet and begin repeating often the brief prayer "Jesus, I trust in You." There are many resources available to help you pray the chaplet,

including the website of the Marian Fathers of the Immaculate Conception of the Blessed Virgin Mary (thedivinemercy.org).

Additional Resources

The Problem of Pain, by C. S. Lewis
Making Sense out of Suffering, by Peter Kreeft

10

Beware the Temptation to Throw in the Towel: Lies about Willpower

A man who governs his passions is master of the world. We must either rule them or be ruled by them. It is better to be the hammer than the anvil.

—St. Dominic[59]

There is nothing more frustrating than those bad habits that you just can't seem to conquer. Maybe it's those favorite foods you'd just as soon give up, but you can't quite make the adjustment. Or maybe it's something else. No matter how hard we try, it seems the old habits so often creep back in just when we think we have them under control.

I don't know about you, but on a bad day, I'm likely to chalk all my failures up to a lack of willpower.

Most of us know in our gut what willpower is. But for the purposes of this discussion, I looked up the definition. According to

---

[59] Quoted in Fr. Joseph Esper, *Saintly Solutions to Life's Common Problems: From Anger, Boredom, and Temptation to Gluttony, Gossip, and Greed* (Manchester, NH: Sophia Institute Press, 2001), 303.

Webster's Dictionary, willpower is "the ability to control yourself: strong determination that allows you to do something difficult."

According to the American Psychological Association,[60] willpower consists of the following:

- the ability to delay gratification, resisting short-term temptations in order to meet long-term goals
- the capacity to override an unwanted thought, feeling, or impulse
- the ability to employ a cognitive system of behavior rather than an emotional system
- conscious, effortful regulation of the self by the self

Essentially, *willpower* is another word for *discipline*. And it enables us to do amazing things. Willpower is what helped Cinthya, a single mother of four, pay off her house in less than two years by giving up everything—including electricity—so she could funnel as many funds as possible toward the achievement of her goal.[61] Willpower is what helped Dick, the father of a paraplegic, push his son, Rick, in a wheelchair to complete (as a team) in 255 triathlons (including 6 ironman triathlons), 72 marathons, and more.[62]

Willpower is what helps us to get up in the morning, to complete our duties, to mind our diet, to manage our money, to go

60 Kirsten Weir, "What You Need to Know About Willpower: The Psychological Science of Self-Control," American Psychological Association, 2012, https://www.apa.org/helpcenter/willpower.pdf.

61 "You'll Need a Tissue for Cinthya's Story," December 5, 2014, YouTube video, 11:18, *The Dave Ramsey Show*, https://www.youtube.com/watch?v=6gsGMoAV90s.

62 "Dick and Rick Hoyt (Team Hoyt)," Triathlon Inspires, https://www.triathloninspires.com/thoytstory.html.

above and beyond, as Cynthia and Dick and countless others have done, and most importantly, to grow in holiness and virtue, as have all the saints before us..

In a nutshell, willpower enables us to sacrifice.

"WILL" YOU BE A VICTIM?

While willpower is essential for success in any endeavor, whether physical or spiritual, conventional wisdom sells it short these days. Rather than fight to assert the will against a penchant for self-indulgence, the world seems to have surrendered altogether, claiming that the will is powerless.

"Experts" have turned against the idea of willpower, arguing that there is no such thing. Even more, to the extent that we think it exists, experts claim we are setting ourselves up for failure; that we lack the wherewithal to tell ourselves no or to ensure that we pursue our goals to their end, and that we would be much better off if we focused on controlling our environments because we have little, if any, control over ourselves.

According to *Nautilus*, an awarding-winning periodical on science, philosophy, and culture, in an article titled "Against Willpower: Willpower Is a Dangerous, Old Idea That Needs to Be Scrapped,"

> willpower may simply be a pre-scientific idea—one that was born from social attitudes and philosophical specula-tion rather than research, and enshrined before rigorous experimental evaluation of it became possible.... These ideas also have a pernicious effect, distracting us from more accurate ways of understanding human psychology and even detracting from our efforts toward meaningful

self-control. The best way forward may be to let go of "willpower" altogether.[63]

Look at this excerpt from an article, originally published in the *Roanoke Times*, that refers to studies that take an even more aggressive stance against the concept of willpower:

> Parents, teachers, coaches and ill-tempered sergeants had insisted that the disciplined exertion of willpower against the baser temptations of sloth, gluttony and other moral frailties was essential to building sufficient character to overcome most adversity. What adversity couldn't be overcome should at least be borne with a modicum of quiet long-suffering, if not grace. Imagine my relief to read of the scientific evidence that willpower is really a myth, especially as it relates to such primal endeavors as dieting. A number of psychologists around the country consider the entire notion of willpower to be just another artifact of quaint but misguided folklore.[64]

It seems everywhere we turn, the devil has another angle to sell. On one hand, he tries to convince us that we can name and claim all our worldly desires; on the other hand, he often tries to convince us that the very will we might need to claim those desires just doesn't even exist.

But there have been subtle messages going on for decades. And they are severely affecting private behavior as well as public

---

[63] Carl Erik Fisher, "Against Willpower: Willpower Is a Dangerous, Old Idea That Needs to Be Scrapped," *Nautilus*, February, 2017, http://nautil.us/issue/45/power/against-willpower.

[64] *Roanoke Times*, "No Such Thing as Willpower?," Mind Power News, http://www.mindpowernews.com/NoWillpower.htm.

policy. Case in point: How long have advocates been insisting that birth control be made readily available in the schools. "Kids are going to do what kids are going to do; they don't have any self-control. The least we can do is help them be prepared." (Arguably, students have lived up to expectations.)

Or what about cities that hand out free hypodermic needles to drug addicts rather than funnel that money toward rehabilitation? "We would be wasting our time and money trying to help addicts change their ways. We may as well just minimize damage from the spread of disease."

What about the idea of guaranteed income? Or even forgiving student loans? These and other ideas were derived under the assumption that people are who they are and cannot practice the virtues of discipline and prudence or learn to control their appetites.

There are other things as well. Pornography is no longer frowned up in many places; open marriages are celebrated; and despite obvious health risks, obesity is now celebrated as a personal choice. The bottom line is that people will do what they will do, so we may as well just validate passions and behavior that would have been unacceptable in years past.

The result of both subtle and not-so-subtle messages about the weakness of the will has been absolutely destructive—what one might call a self-fulfilling prophecy. Consider a few statistics:

- According to the Centers for Disease Control (CDC), over 70 percent of Americans are overweight, with nearly 40 percent of them being obese.[65]

---

[65] "Obesity and Overweight," National Center for Health Statistics, https://www.cdc.gov/nchs/fastats/obesity-overweight.htm.

- Ashley Madison, a website that caters to married people looking for affairs, boasts a client list of fifty-four million.[66]
- Half of older Americans have absolutely no retirement savings.[67]
- As of December 2018, consumer debt reached a whopping $13.3 trillion.[68]

When it comes to willpower, the danger of denying it lies not merely in the physical realm. Willpower is a God-given gift and is necessary if we want to grow in holiness. According to Pew Research, across our nation, the number of people who pray and attend religious services consistently has dropped 3 percent across the board since 2007. And younger people observe religious practices significantly less than older populations do.[69]

People point to this or that reason for declining participation in Christian churches, but isn't there likely a huge correlation between the lack of interest in religion and the decrease in

---

[66] Ashley May, "Husband Cheating? Ashley Madison Says Member Signups Spiked in These Cities Last Year," *USA Today*, June 22, 2018, https://www.usatoday.com/story/news/nation-now/2018/06/22/cities-most-ashley-madison-accounts-cheating-husbands/720864002/.

[67] Ben Steverman, "Half of Older Americans Have Nothing in Retirement Savings," Bloomberg, March 26, 2019, https://www.bloomberg.com/news/articles/2019-03-26/almost-half-of-older-americans-have-zero-in-retirement-savings.

[68] Matt Tatham, "Consumer Debt Reaches $13 Trillion in Q4 2018," Experian, March 26, 2019, https://www.experian.com/blogs/ask-experian/research/consumer-debt-study/.

[69] "Three-Point Drop in Share of Public Reporting Weekly Worship Attendance," Pew Research Center, October 29, 2015, https://www.pewforum.org/2015/11/03/u-s-public-becoming-less-religious/pf-2015-11-03_rls_ii-40/.

control of our baser desires? My point here is not that one has caused the other; but perhaps all areas have been driven by the deeper message that we've been hearing in the world: — that we cannot control ourselves; that we are destined to live with our powerlessness and must simply go along for the ride, despite that fact that both we and our progeny must find ways to cope with the devastation left in our wake. In this culture of hedonism, the call for vigilance in virtually every area has waned.

Perhaps willpower *is* a prescientific idea as asserted above; but only insofar as Adam and Eve existed before the scientific method. The will is one of the things that separates humans from animals, and willpower is nothing more than the assertion and acknowledgment that your will is free. You, as a child of God, have been given the ability — or the power — to determine for yourself how you will respond to your feelings, your loved ones, your environment, and your God in any given moment. God gave you free will out of respect and generosity, allowing you the opportunity to choose Him, rather than forcing your allegiance to Him through His almighty power. That choice is not a momentary decision but consists of countless daily, moment-by-moment decisions to pick up your crosses; to grow in holiness, love, and virtue; to participate in prayer and the sacraments, cooperating with the grace of God to become a better version of yourself. Willpower is something you should cherish as a great gift. And you surrender that power at your own peril.

When you deny power over your will, you make yourself a victim of your passions. You become helpless in the face of emotional and environmental factors. The culture seems to perpetuate this victimization. Many claim to be subject to their circumstances — whatever they may be — and they argue that change is just not possible for the long term. How often do you hear, "That's just the way I am"?

I am so thankful that we have the wisdom of the saints to guide us regarding matters like this, rather than the latest psychobabble of the culture.

A HALF-BAKED WILL

St. Augustine had plenty to say about the will. And to be perfectly clear, he *did not* say that there was no such thing as willpower. But he did have an explanation for the problem of giving up those pesky bad habits and of our failure to cement the good ones. In his book *The Confessions* is a chapter called "The Two Wills." In it he claims that the problem isn't that the mind cannot control the body. The problem is that the mind doesn't really want to change the body. There is this little problem of compelling the will to be ruled.[70] On the one hand, we may will ourselves to break a habit or to develop a new habit; but on the other hand, we secretly like the status quo. There is something in that bad habit that is comforting, rewarding, or just plain enjoyable. We like the idea of developing new habits but not enough for our wills to be all in. We like the idea of sacrifice, but we don't like the pain that comes with it. This is why we don't change. This is why we fail to offer ourselves at the next level.

That said, boiling everything down to helplessness on our part is not useful. Playing the victim card is a losing battle—especially when we desire change. We can change our habits. We can make sacrifices. We can do great things. And God will give

---

[70] *The Confessions of Saint Augustine*, trans. John K. Ryan (New York: Image Books, 1960), 196–197.

us the grace to accomplish them, provided we can master our wills in the process. How do we do this? One choice at a time.

A quick look around reveals that people buck their circumstances all the time—to the extent that they refuse to don the mantle of victimhood. The human capacity for self-determination is virtually without limit, provided man does not surrender his ability to choose.

Rest assured that your will is intact. In fact, according to Archbishop Fulton Sheen, it is the only thing you have that is truly yours:

> There is only one thing in the world that is definitely and absolutely your own, and that is your will. Health, power, possessions and honor can all be snatched from you, but your will is irrevocably your own, even in hell. Hence, nothing really matters in life, except what you do with your will.[71]

CHOICES

Despite what the media says, despite what the "professionals" in the world of psychology say, regardless of what your best friend tells you, you can put down that doughnut. You can lose that last ten pounds. You can find time to exercise today. You can control you temper. You can save for retirement. You can find time to pray. You can grow in virtue. You can become a saint!

In order to obtain Heaven, two things are required: God's grace and your will. The world has done a great job of convincing us that neither exists. But the world is wrong.

---

[71] Fulton J. Sheen, *Seven Words of Jesus and Mary* (Liguori, MO: Liguori/Triumph, 2001), 25.

In every moment of every day, your choices matter. They matter when it comes to your peace and happiness in this world, and they matter for your eternal happiness in the next. You have choices because in His goodness, God provided you with free will and the ability to choose your own destiny. He did this, that you might choose to follow Him. He desires for you to know Him, to love Him, and to serve Him of your own volition. He will not force His way upon you. The will is absolutely key for your ability to make any kind of offering to God. It is the key to enduring suffering, growing in virtue, and achieving sanctity. The will is also critical for accomplishing material goals, because in very practical ways, what is good for your soul is also good for your body.

Sadly, in the real world our choices don't always match up with our desires. A weak will can mean the death of good intentions, so that too often we do the exact thing we were determined not to do, or we fail to do the very thing we were committed to doing only moments before. Consider the last time you vowed to keep your cool, only to lose your temper when the going got tough; or when you were sure this would be the day you would wake up early; but the bed just felt too good when the alarm sounded this morning. Or what about that commitment you made to pray the Rosary every evening? Or to attend daily Mass? What about all the energy you spent planning a daily routine that would help you to grow in holiness, only to go back to your old ways before the end of the first week?

Rest assured you are not alone. This struggle has existed since Adam and Eve strolled through the Garden of Eden. St. Paul recorded his own struggle in his letter to the Romans: "I can will what is right, but I cannot do it. For I do not do the good I want, but the evil I do not want is what I do." (Rom. 7:18–19).

You may desire virtue, but when you give in to poor choices, you order the will toward vice, and vice becomes easier. If you do not remain vigilant by weeding out bad habits before they take root, they are sure to overtake the good. Unfortunately, self-indulgence is the wider, often more pleasant path (at least in the short term). Self-discipline requires focus, perseverance, and conscientiousness.

It is not enough to keep your vices, or bad habits, under control. You must pursue virtue, or develop good habits, in order to make progress in the spiritual life. As we all know, this is easier said than done. The saints have confronted this battle, and they have implored Christians to remain on guard. St. Francis de Sales says this:

> We must in no way be surprised to find self-love in us, for it never leaves us. Like a fox it sleeps sometimes, then all of a sudden leaps on the chickens; for which reason we must constantly keep watch on it, and patiently and very quietly defend ourselves from it.[72]

But my will is weak, you say. Yes, I'm sure it is. There is only one perfect will. And while we share in God's image, our fallen nature, like a leaden weight, seems destined to keep us from soaring to great heights. But your will is there. And God's grace is the chisel that will cut away the lead; for through Him all things are possible (see Matt. 19:26). And His "power is made perfect in weakness" (2 Cor. 12:9).

---

[72] St. Francis de Sales, *Thy Will Be Done: Fifty-Eight Letters to Souls Troubled by Problems That Afflict Each of Us Today: Anger, Frustration, Grief and Sickness, Difficulties in Praying, and Even Lack of Faith—with Wise, Practical Remedies for Each* (Manchester: Sophia Institute Press, 1995), 195.

THE LOST ART OF SACRIFICE

THE WILL TO TRAIN THE WILL

It may be a challenge to get started on the path to discipline. But just as you must take pains to ensure a well-formed conscience, you must also train your will. That can be a challenge—particularly when you've become a little permissive with yourself. Once you allow yourself license to pursue pleasure on a whim, neglecting boundaries here or there, it can be difficult to get back on the narrow path. But make no mistake: it is doable. You may need to take one step at a time, but little by little, you can overcome poor habits. Start small. Attention to those seemingly trivial habits is critical. It is from there that you can grow to achieve strength and character in the "big" things and can lead others to do the same. St. Josemaría Escrivá says:

> Will-power. A very important quality. Don't disregard the little things which are really never futile or trivial. For by the constant practice of repeated self-denial in little things, with God's grace you will increase in strength and manliness of character. In that way you'll first become master of yourself, and then a guide and a leader: to compel, to urge, to draw others with your example and with your word and with your knowledge and with your power.[73]

St. Josemaría Escrivá demonstrates that there is a way to strengthen the will. But the *Catechism* provides a prescription: progress in virtue, knowledge of the good and severe self-discipline (ascesis) (see 1734).

The more we unite ourselves to Christ, the more we desire what He desires, the more we emulate Him, the more power we

[73] St. Josemaría Escrivá, *The Way* (New York: Scepter, 1982), 6.

will attain over our wills. Willpower is necessary for happiness in this life and is absolutely critical for any kind of growth toward the next.

Not only does our health depend on our ability to see the devil's lies for what they are; our salvation depends on it as well. For how can I unite my will to God's if I believe I have no power to do so? God is faithful. He has provided us with everything we need to pursue sanctity. And the gift of the will is a necessary component:

> God does not require of us the martyrdom of the body; He requires only the martyrdom of the heart and the will.[74]

Don't buy the lie. Don't shun the greatest ally in your pursuit of sanctity. Don't dismiss the most valuable tool in the control of your destiny. Little by little, you can train yourself in virtue. Willpower begins with small, seemingly insignificant sacrifices. You can live a life of sacrifice by starting small, trusting God, and allowing His grace to take you beyond your weakness.

CULTIVATING THE ART OF SACRIFICE

Contrary to popular belief—as exposed in the *Atlantic* article that said, "There is no such thing as free will"—you are not an animal. One of the things that makes you human is your ability to choose. Recognizing that you have options is powerful. Knowing that you can make decisions consciously but that

---

[74] As quoted in Jill Haak Adels, *The Wisdom of the Saints: An Anthology* (New York: Oxford University Press, 1987), 78.

falling into a habit is also a decision (albeit a passive one) is an important step.

Action

1. *Recognize that you have free will.* Take an inventory of all the decisions you've effectively made today. Now slow down for the rest of the day and notice everything you do that requires a decision, whether you are going to walk up the stairs, turn on the TV, scroll through Facebook, raise your voice, read a book, fold laundry, stick to your shopping list, exercise, or play with your kids. Recognizing that you have to rule your day is an important step toward taking control.

2. *Exercise your will as you would exercise a muscle.* As with any other exercise, start small. You can't walk into a gym and start bench-pressing three hundred pounds. If you want to make serious progress, start small and gradually improve.

   A great way to get started training your will is to decide what time to get up every day and not to let yourself hit the snooze button. Gradually, as you master your wake-up time, it should be easier to master your bedtime — after all, you'll probably get tired earlier if you are waking up earlier every day. Build off that first exercise. For example, in the spiritual life, consider signing up for a committed Holy Hour. Or decide to attend a daily Mass. And then do it. Whatever you do, start small and master that exercise before you add another. Otherwise you risk burning yourself out and ending up back where you are today.

3. *Find your* why *for any decision.* Love of God is the perfect *why*, but as with Confession, even imperfect motives will

help (see CCC 1451–1453). These might include love of a family member, love of community, or love of your own body as at temple of the Holy Spirit. Any *why* that draws you closer to God or neighbor is a good *why*. Anything that does not should cause you to reconsider your goals.

4. *Curb your passions with virtues.* When you want to eliminate something in your life, the only way to keep it from flowing back into your life is to fill the hole left behind with something else. That's where virtue comes in!! Follow the habits of Benjamin Franklin, who made a strict practice of focusing his efforts on one virtue for two weeks at a time. He would make a list of specific things he would do to practice and follow through during that period. When two weeks were up, he would move on to the next virtue on his list, making his way through a cycle of thirteen virtues twice each year.[75]

5. *Be patient with yourself when you fail.* St. Bernard learned this lesson the hard way with those under his direction.[76] He had such a fervent zeal for souls that he treated every infraction with extreme harshness and his results were abominable, as his great passion for perfection backfired. Rather than inspiring progress, his severity held his novices back. Eventually Bernard realized his mistake and began to approach those under his guidance with the utmost patience and tenderness, and his efforts bore much fruit. The same will be true for you. If you berate yourself

---

[75] Benjamin Franklin, *The Autobiography and Other Writings* (New York: Penguin Classics, 1986), 182–184.

[76] St. Francis de Sales, *An Introduction to the Devout Life* (Rockford, IL: TAN Books, 1994), 111.

for every error, you will be much less likely to find success. Humbly acknowledge your faults before God, and seek His grace as you begin anew. Only in a state of true piety will you succeed.

Additional Resources

The Way, by St. Josemaría Escrivá

Learning the Virtues That Lead You to God, by Romano Guardini

Part 3

The Art of Sacrifice

*Then I said, "Lo, I have come
to do thy will, O God."*

—Hebrews 10:7

Once we get past all the lies that undermine our desire to sacrifice, the real work begins. First, we must look ourselves in the mirror and reconsider the path we're on. We must ask, "Do I want to steep myself in the culture, or do I want to steep myself in God's grace? Do I want to engage in self-love, or do I want to love God?" In many ways, the two paths are like oil and water: they don't mix. Our answer may seem obvious today, but these are questions that we must ask ourselves over and over again because our hearts are not stagnant, and they often become distracted in ways that require intentional review and redirection.

Remember, Christ wants all of you. He doesn't just want the hour you spend at Mass on Sunday. He wants every moment of every day. What are you willing to give Him?

Please note: Since part 3 of this book is more practical in nature, you will see that, instead of being given in a closing section to each chapter, practical suggestions for cultivating the art of sacrifice are interwoven throughout the text.

11

Dispositions That Make Way for Sacrifice

Why stoop to drink from the puddles of worldly
consolations if you can satisfy your thirst with
waters that spring up into life everlasting?

—St. Josemaría Escrivá[77]

As you weigh your passion for Christ, ask yourself how much you embody the following dispositions, each of which is critical to the art of sacrifice. No matter how weak you may be today, with prayer and reflection you can learn to cultivate each disposition in God's time. Please note that while these ideas receive little fanfare in the world, in the world of grace, they are everything.

HORROR OF SIN

Flannery O'Connor had a knack for shocking readers through her use of the grotesque, often using repugnant images to make her point. Her stories graphically demonstrated the powerful hold that sin can have on us and the explosive nature of grace at key moments in life.

[77] *The Way*, 49.

In her short story "A Good Man Is Hard to Find," O'Connor illustrates that rather than have a horror of sin, deep down, we actually *like* it. We treat sin like a cozy old blanket — we snuggle into it, becoming very comfortable in our bad habits and our selfish choices. O'Connor features a particularly vivid image of our affinity for sin through her description of a monkey eating fleas: "The Children ran outside into the white sunlight and looked at the monkey in the lacey chinaberry tree. He was busy catching fleas on himself and biting each one carefully between his teeth as if it were a delicacy."[78]

The realization that the monkey and the fleas represent us and our sin is almost physically sickening. Can you think of a more repulsive image to illustrate our relationship to sin?

The plot of the story features a grandmother, who, like many of us, is a first-class hypocrite. While she puts on Christian "airs," her behavior leaves much to be desired. O'Connor contrasts her unattractive personality with her prim and proper appearance: "The old lady settled comfortably, removing her white cotton gloves.... Her collars and cuffs were white organdy trimmed with lace and at her neckline she had pinned a purple spray of violets containing a sachet. In case of an accident, anyone seeing her dead on the highway would know at once that she was a lady."[79] While the grandmother carries herself as a proper woman, throughout the story her motives and actions attest to her depravity. Yet she is so oblivious to her own sin that she seems to have mistaken it for virtue.

At the climax of the story, the family, including the grandmother, encounters three criminals who have escaped prison.

---

[78] Flannery O'Connor, *A Good Man Is Hard to Find and Other Stories* (San Diego: Harcourt Brace & Company, 1981), 1.

[79] Ibid., 5.

One by one, family members are shot in the forest, until the grandmother is the only one left. Realizing the end is near, she suddenly becomes the Christian she has always portrayed herself to be. Over and over again, she invites the leader to pray, and in the end she becomes a conduit of grace, reaching out to him with great sincerity. Unfortunately, he rejects her attempt. In fact, he recoils, shooting her three times, until she "half lay in a puddle of blood with her legs crossed under her like a child's and her face smiling up at the cloudless sky."[80]

In commentary on her work, O'Connor says, "This heroine of this story, the Grandmother, is in the most significant position life offers the Christian. She is facing death. And to all appearances she, like the rest of us, is not too well prepared for it. She would like to see the event postponed. Indefinitely."[81]

Unfortunately, it takes facing imminent death for the grandmother to be aware of her need for redemption and to be open to receiving grace. In fact, upon her death, the villain even comments, "She would have been a good woman ... if it had been somebody there to shoot her every minute of her life."[82]

Is this true for you? Will it take facing death for you to flee from sin in abject horror and persevere in virtue? If so, remind yourself on a daily basis of the always looming, absolutely inevitable nature of death. Death will come for you when you least expect it, so be ever on guard against the dangers of sin.

Venerable Louis of Granada tells us that the only way to develop a horror of sin is to receive grace—not merely in the

---

[80] Ibid., 22.

[81] Flannery O'Connor, *Mystery and Manners: Occasional Prose* (New York: Farrar, Straus & Giroux, 1970), 110.

[82] O'Connor, *A Good Man*, 22.

hour of death but as often as we can. As Christians, we must take advantage of every conduit of grace available to us to fix a horror of sin deep within our souls. Those conduits include the sacraments, prayer, and a firm resolution to keep our eyes on eternity. Venerable Louis advises us:

> He who desires to walk resolutely in the same path must strive to imitate them [the saints] by fixing this resolution deep in his soul. Appreciating things at their true value, he must prefer the friendship of God to all treasures of earth; he must unhesitatingly sacrifice perishable joys for delights that will be eternal. To accomplish this must be the end of all his actions; the object of all his prayers; the fruit he seeks in frequenting the sacraments; the profit he derives from sermons and pious reading; the lesson he should learn from the beauty and harmony of the world, and from all creatures. This will be the happy result of Our Savior's Passion and all the other works of love which He unceasingly performs. They will inspire him with a horror of offending the good Master who has done so much for him. Finally, this holy fear and firm resolution will be the mark of his progress in virtue.[83]

If we fail to follow this advice, we'll lose our ability to recognize sin in our midst. As O'Connor warns, "The devil's greatest wile, Baudelaire had said, is to convince us that he does not exist."[84]

To pursue a genuine life of sacrifice, we must approach God with an open heart, a heart that is available to Him. How can

---

[83] Venerable Louis of Granada, *The Sinner's Guide* (Rockford, IL: TAN Books, 1985), 254–255.

[84] O'Connor, *Mystery and Manners*, 112.

our hearts be available to God if we have an attachment to sin? And in order to develop a love for God that will allow us to follow Him through a life of sacrifice, we must not only get rid of any attachment to sin, but we must absolutely abhor it. For only a pure heart can enter into the Heart of Jesus. Any mark of transgression is a lesion of separation that must be healed in the sacrament of Confession.

The Virtue of Purity

The only heart that can be perfectly united to Christ is a pure heart. Approach anything that might keep you from that perfect union as anathema. Purity is a very effective weapon to use in thrashing any secret affinity you may have to sin — not only mortal sin but even venial sin. Pursue purity so that you may develop an intimate relationship with Our Lord, one that will help you to unite your sacrifices to His out of deep and abiding love, rather than out of duty.

According to St. John Paul II, "Having a pure heart means being a new person, restored to life in communion with God and with all creation by the redemptive love of Christ, brought back to that communion which is our original destiny."[85] A pure heart is one that has been restored to the intimate union experienced by Adam and Eve before the Fall. Holy purity will remove any burden of weight from your soul, allowing you to fly to your Heavenly Father in love.

Set aside some uninterrupted time to perform a thorough examination of conscience. Follow up by making a good confession.

---

[85] St. John Paul II, Homily (Sandomierz, June 12, 1999), no. 2, http://www.vatican.va/content/john-paul-ii/en/travels/1999/documents/hf_jp-ii_hom_12061999_sandomierz.html.

Then spend time in prayer and ask God to help you develop an absolute horror of any kind of sin, preserving you in holy purity, so that you may have room in your heart to develop a love for Him above all things.

A STRONG DESIRE TO HAVE
A FERVENT LOVE FOR JESUS

Recently I went shopping with my nine-year-old daughter, and she found a backpack she just had to have. When she realized I was not going to buy it for her, she became bound and determined to find some way to get her hands on it as soon as possible. All the way home, she discussed nothing but the backpack — the size, the color, its sheer softness, and the convenience of its many pockets, both inside and out.

The first thing she did when we got home was to find her wallet, count all her change, and secure it in a baggie labeled for the prize she was seeking. Once she figured out how much she still needed, she began to devise a plan. First, she reminded me that I still owed her three dollars for picking weeds a few weeks earlier. Then she did what most people do when they want money: she went to work. Sometimes her grandmother hires her to pick up after her dog, so she called her first. Once she secured that job, she offered to do chores for her siblings for a nominal fee. She called her dad at work and offered her services for any odd jobs that weren't already on her chore list (we don't give our kids allowances). For the next few days, she dreamed, she planned, she worked, and she counted. Her passion didn't let up until we headed back to the store with her funds in hand.

That's what I think of when I think of desire. It is passionate, active, determined, and disciplined.

The word *desire* is a funny thing because, like love, it has been expanded to cover an array of situations. Essentially it has become a synonym for *want*. For example, you may desire that your mother live forever and never age. Maybe you desire to visit Venice. Or you might have a desire to renovate your bathroom. Some of these desires are clearly out of your control. Others may be within your control, but then the question becomes: Does the desire inspire movement on your part toward its achievement? In other words, will you do anything about it?

Desire is defined in general as "a movement of the soul toward the good that is absent."[86] So desire is different from the acquisition of the good. And it is also different from the pursuit of the good. But there are two kinds of desire. One is merely a feeling, a passionate inner drive toward something that is lacking. The other is a movement of the will toward the good in question. The latter kind of desire is rational, and in the case of the desire to have a fervent love for Jesus, it is also a supernatural desire, and as such, it is influenced by divine grace.

The fact is that a desire to love Jesus does not stem from you. From all eternity, God has been with you and has sought union with you: "I have loved you with an everlasting love; therefore I have continued my faithfulness to you" (Jer. 31:3). Given that this invitation was first offered by God and has somehow kindled in you a great motivation to draw closer to Him, to love Him in return with all the love you can possibly muster in your human nature, and then even more via His supernatural grace, you can rest assured that He will answer the desire of your heart.

---

[86] Very Reverend Adolphe Tanquerey, *The Spiritual Life* (Belgium: Society of St. John the Evangelist, 1930), 205.

But what if right now, your desire to have a fervent love for Christ is not that strong? There are several things you can do. First, if you lack a desire to place your love in God, then you may be placing it somewhere else. With yourself? With something in the world? Ask yourself what's keeping you from desiring — with passion, determination, drive, and discipline — a fervent love of Christ? Often our lack of love boils down to nothing more than selfishness. In *The 12 Steps to Holiness and Salvation*, St. Alphonsus Liguori says,

> Our heart cannot exist without love; it will either love God or creatures. If it does not love creatures, it certainly will love God. In order to become holy we must therefore banish from our heart all that is not for God. When anyone came to the Fathers in the desert and desired to be received by them he was asked: "Do you bring an empty heart that it may be filled by the Holy Ghost?" And they were right, for a heart that is filled with the things of earth has no room for the love of God. He who brings a vessel filled with earth to the spring will never be able to fill it with water until he empties it of the earth with which it is filled.[87]

If your heart is full of love for something other than God, you must empty it. Get rid of anything in your life that keeps you from God.

God greatly desires that you love Him with all your heart, mind, soul, and strength. Because that is so strongly His desire, if you beg Him by your prayers to inspire you, He will surely answer

---

[87] St. Alphonsus Liguori, *The 12 Steps to Holiness and Salvation* (Charlotte, NC: TAN Books, 2010), 73.

you. Ask the Lord, simply and often, "Help me to empty myself of anything that hinders my desire to love You as You deserve to be loved." If you already desire a great love for God, then bask in the hope of that intimate relationship that both you and God will continue to pursue.

The Virtue of Gratitude

One way to deepen your desire for love of God is to grow in the virtue of gratitude. Before we can love God, we need to understand how much He loves us as well as how much He has done for us and how much we depend on Him. After all, "we love, because he first loved us" (1 John 4:19). According to Venerable Louis of Granada, "one of the greatest impulses that move the heart to love is the recognition of benefits received."[88] He says that although love is good in its own right, often we tend to love our own good. To the extent that we are grateful to God, we will desire to have a fervent love for Him. St. John XXIII understood this well. He reminded himself of his proper place before God, as well as how grateful he was for all that God had done for him:

> I am nothing. Everything I possess, my being, my life, understanding, will and memory—all were given me by God, so all belong to Him. Twenty short years ago all that I see around me was already here; the same sun, moon and stars, the same mountain, seas, deserts, beasts, plants and men; everything was proceeding in its appointed way under the watchful eyes of Divine Providence. And I? I was not here....

[88] Venerable Louis of Granada, O.P., *Summa of the Christian Life*, vol. 1 (Rockford, IL: Tan Books, 1979), 216.

And you, O God, with a wonderful gesture of love, you who are from the beginning and before all time, you drew me forth from my nothingness, you gave me being, life, a soul, in fact all the faculties of my body and spirit; you opened my eyes to this light which sheds its radiance around me, you created me. So you are my Master and I am your creature. I am nothing without you; indeed, if at every moment you did not support me I should slip back whence I came, into nothingness. This is what I am. And yet I am boastful and display with pride before the eyes of God all the blessings He has showered on me, as if they were my own. Oh what a fool I am! "For what have you that you did not receive? If you then received it, why do you boast as if it were not a gift?" (1 Cor. 4:7).

. . . What am I but an ant or a grain of sand? Why do I put myself up so proudly? Arrogance, pride, self-esteem! What am I set in this world to do? To serve God.[89]

Spend time each day contemplating your obligation to love Our Lord, and ask Him to enkindle in your heart a love for Him. He absolutely will answer that prayer.

A TRUE SENSE OF MORTIFICATION

Many years ago I was listening to a Catholic radio show the Friday before Mother's Day, and people were calling in to pay tribute to the many wonderful attributes they had witnessed in their moms. One caller stopped me in my tracks. She told how she and her sisters had loved to bake with their mom when growing up. There

---

[89] Pope John XXIII, *Journal of a Soul*, 64–65.

was not a cookie their mother didn't like, and she baked all the time. But this caller recalled so clearly early in 1973, when her mother heard that the Supreme Court ruled that a woman had a "right" to an abortion. On that day, her mother declared that she would not eat another cookie until the ruling was overturned. The caller said her mother never mentioned that case again. But even into her twilight years, when her children offered her a cookie at holiday gatherings, thinking surely enough time had gone by, or when anyone else offered her one, she would always politely refuse. For the rest of her life, her children never saw her eat another cookie.

This daughter explained that she had learned nothing so powerful in life as the trust in God that her mother had demonstrated. This woman had offered what to her seemed a small contribution toward overturning the diabolical evil that had come over our country, and she remained committed to the very end. It's hard to imagine the graces that have and will continue to be poured out upon the world as a result of her quiet act of love.

Don't Count the Cost

If a desire to love God is a necessary disposition, then a true sense of mortification means that I have a willingness to put my money where my mouth is. The desire to love is necessary. But that desire to love must be coupled with the desire to act on that love. This idea goes back to the very heart of this book — Christ's call to His would-be disciples:

> If any man would come after me, let him *deny himself* and take up his cross and follow me. (Matt. 16:24, emphasis mine)

Sacrifice is not primarily about feelings. All sacrifice costs something. The cost may be low, or it may be high, depending on the circumstances. Whatever the case, the amount that we will be able to give is directly proportionate to the amount that we are willing to give up.

There are two kinds of mortification. There is exterior morti-fication, which is the one we most often associate with the term. This is the kind of mortification that denies or limits the flesh for the sake of some spiritual good, such as my friend's fasting for her husband's conversion. The second kind is interior mortification, wherein you repress selfish affections of the mind and heart;[90] for example, when you bite your tongue rather than defend yourself in the face of a snide comment, or when you smile in the face of frustration rather than letting it all hang out.

Both exterior and interior mortification are invaluable with regard to the strengthening of the will, the discipline of character, and the supernatural graces afforded through our intentional efforts. Most importantly, mortification is a practical means of fighting against one of the greatest hindrances to a love of God —love of *self*. If we desire to love God, we can do so only to the extent that we are willing to overcome our passions, arm our wills against temptations and maintain a constant vigilance over the self.

Our bodies and souls need to work together toward our sanc-tification. But if we are not careful, the passions of our bodies —sloth, lust, gluttony, and the like—will undermine the desires of our souls. This is why willpower is so important. To live the art of sacrifice, the soul must become the master and the body its

[90] Fr. John Croiset, S.J., *The Devotion to the Sacred Heart* (Charlotte, NC: TAN Books, 1988), 130.

servant. This requires a willingness and a plan of action for the mortification of the self. If we do not set about overcoming our passions, they will sneak up on us and show themselves when we least expect it. We must keep constant watch.

St. Josemaría Escrivá founded the world-renowned ministry Opus Dei (Latin for "Work of God") to facilitate for all people the pursuit of holiness through our vocations by sanctifying our daily work. He taught that our daily work includes the way of the Cross, because within our vocations we have ample opportunity to sanctify ourselves by uniting our wills to the will of the Father. In his masterful little book *The Way*, Escrivá offers many practical tips on mortification, such as these:[91]

- The appropriate word you left unsaid; the joke you didn't tell; the cheerful smile for those who bother you; that silence when you're unjustly accused; your kind conversation with people you find boring and tactless; the daily effort to overlook one irritating detail or another in those who live with you ... this, with perseverance, is indeed solid interior mortification
- Choose mortification that doesn't mortify others.
- The eyes! Through them much wickedness enters into the soul. How many experiences like David's! If you guard your eyes, you'll be assured of guarding your heart.
- Everything that doesn't lead you to God is an obstacle. Tear it out and cast it far from you.

The possibilities for mortification are endless. Without a willingness and even a desire to dive in, it will be very difficult for us to unite ourselves to Christ. Archbishop Fulton Sheen uses

---

[91] St. Josemaría Escrivá, *The Way of the Cross* (New York: Scepter Publishers, 2004), 57–65.

this simple example of a pen: If you pick up a pen and decide to write the word *God*, and your pen is a willing instrument in your hands, as is generally the case, you will be able to write the word as you desire and the pen will have perfectly served its purpose. But say that pen had a mind of its own, a will that wanted something other than to write the word *God*. What if, when you picked up that pen to write the word *God*, the pen decided to write *dog*? Well in that case, your pen was rather useless to you. And so it is with us.[92]

To the extent that I insist on making my own way, I cannot possibly pursue the art of sacrifice, for I am unwilling to deny myself. But to the extent that I am striving to conquer my will so that I may offer myself to my Heavenly Father, I will be an instrument in His hands, and He will accomplish great things in the world through my sacrifice.

This is where we can drastically improve our lives. Every time we deny ourselves something that we might otherwise enjoy, provided it is done out of love, we are not only teaching ourselves discipline, but we are directing our eyes to Heaven, reminding ourselves that this life is not our end. Our sacrifice bears witness in our own hearts to our faith. At the moment, we may not indulge in sleeping in or in that extra TV show, but in offering to give up these things to God, whether for love of Him, for the salvation of souls, or for some other purpose, the grace that flows from these small acts of the will is more powerful than we can imagine.

Are you overwhelmed by the practical, boots-on-the-ground concept of mortification? No need. If you are willing, He is

---

[92] Fulton Sheen, *A Retreat for Everyone*, Talk 8, "The Incarnation," Bishop Sheen Today, https://www.bishopsheentoday.com/listen-to-sheen/a-retreat-for-everyone/.

ready. Place your desire into His hands, and He will take it from there.

Virtue of Generosity

One way to develop a true sense of mortification is to grow in the virtue of generosity. A closed fist cannot offer a gift, but neither can it receive one. To receive God's grace and be able to cooperate with His call, we must open our minds, our hearts, and our hands. Growing in the virtue of generosity is a great way also to expand our willingness to mortify ourselves. The more we are willing to share of ourselves, the less attached we will become to this world and the easier it will be to forgo material comforts, to be silent rather than comment in the face of perceived attacks, and to be happy with less. In that regard, generosity is a great friend to our sense of mortification. It allows us to release our grasp on material pleasures in favor of something far greater: our sanctification.

Generosity is a great antidote to greed, which is one of the seven deadly sins. But even more, generosity helps us to emulate God Almighty, who is the epitome of generosity. Generosity helps us to be merciful, as God is merciful. Rather than focus on our own needs, wants, and desires, generosity helps us to extend ourselves in someone else's direction, whether with heart or hand. That someone else in our lives includes the entire Body of Christ. When it comes to developing a true sense of mortification, our willingness to give can expand to the spiritual when we recognize that our prayers, fasting, and other offerings for the greater good have value for both the living and the dead. No doubt God will use our small (or great) gifts of sacrifice to save souls and to change the world.

AN INTERIOR LIFE THAT ALLOWS
FOR RECOLLECTION

Several years ago I took advantage of a much-needed opportunity to attend a two-day mothers' retreat and was afforded the privilege of sleeping in the guest quarters of a convent. To this day I recall neither the theme of the retreat, nor any of the speakers or topics of discussion. I cannot even tell you where the retreat was held or who attended.

But I can tell you about my room.

It was small. Sparsely furnished, it contained a twin bed and a desk with a chair. Covering the bed was a simple white bedspread that hung to the floor and a cotton pillow housed in a plain white pillowcase. The modest desk was neat and clean, and the mismatched wooden chair appeared to have been one from an inexpensive dining set. The only adornment in the entire room was a wooden crucifix, which hung above the desk, within direct sight of the bed. That was it.

Within that room, I felt a breathtaking amount of peace. I distinctly remember thinking, "This is all I need. Everything else is superfluous."

Interior recollection is possible only for a soul that lacks distraction. This disposition is critical to the spiritual life because only a soul capable of recollection can truly unite itself to Christ. A soul capable of recollection is able to *listen* to Our Lord and to develop an intimate relationship with Him rooted in the deepest recesses of the heart. If you want to contemplate the existence of God, His great majesty, and the meaning and purpose of life, you must set aside time and space for recollection.

Obviously, the sisters at the convent where my retreat was held recognized the need to remove as much distraction as possible. Would someone who walked into your home experience a calm refuge amid the storms of the world? Does your home lend itself to a simple, peaceful, prayerful, joy-filled existence? Or is it a cacophony of visible and audible noise? What about your personal disposition? Do you spend ample time in silence each day, lifting your heart and mind to God? Or do you busy yourself with lists of projects and activities a mile long, occupying your days with the incessant spinning of plates in the air and the never-ending worry that one or more will spin free and then everything will come crashing down around you?

The Virtue of Simplicity

Material and spiritual simplicity are absolutely necessary for living a recollected life. Of course, if you are blessed with a spouse and children, I'm not suggesting that you abandon your family and hole yourself up in a convent for the rest of your days. Perhaps it would be better to simplify your environment, and better yet to simplify your soul. Is your home filled with decorative tchotchkes that you have to dust day in and day out in order to keep it looking like a model home? Is your schedule so busy that you spend hours a day running from here to there, chasing the culture with all your (and your kids') activities? Is your soul occupied with worries and concerns about this or that and these and those? Or do you take time to reflect and to cast your cares upon your Heavenly Father, remaining tranquil and unharmed?

What about your interactions with the rest of the world? Do you spend your time watching TV or scrolling online? Social media can be especially problematic. Whether we desire to keep track of loved ones, get in touch with long-lost friends, follow the news, or even stay abreast of the best in Catholic blogging, social media promises to serve that desire for knowledge that rests in the depths of each and every human soul. Sadly, that desire can never be satisfied because the targets are ever-changing, and they require our constant attention just to keep up.

Ask yourself how all that entertainment and constant striving ranks against a peaceful, recollected soul now and against life for all eternity? Sometimes even doing good things such as watching inspirational shows or keeping up with old friends can cause problems when they take what little time you have available to spend with God.

Recollection is not merely about overcoming distractions. It's more about overcoming the world itself. It's about overcoming exterior (or interior) obstacles, infringements, abuses, inconveniences, or situations with the interior joy that comes from knowing Christ and trusting Him. Recollection offers peace and joy even in the midst of trial. It helps us to keep our mind and heart rightly ordered, focused not so much on things that are seen, but on those that are unseen.

Relationships take time, space, and commitment. Now is a good time to reevaluate all three. Set time aside for God three times a day—morning, noon, and night. Start small if necessary, but do commit. Over time, you will find yourself adding time to your preliminary rule. Set aside space for your time with God. Simplify that space, even if it's just a little corner with a chair or a kneeler, maybe a candle and a crucifix. Keep your Bible nearby for spiritual reading. Over time, beginning in that corner, work your way out, simplifying your surroundings little by little. A simplified environment will help curb material attachments as well as enhance your ability to remain thoroughly recollected at all times.

12

Penance and Mortification

We become like angels when we strive to do God's will,
but we become like animals when we seek to
gratify our senses. Either the soul must subject
the body or the body will make the soul its slave.

—St. Alphonsus Liguori[93]

Let us delve deeper into the disposition that enables us to pursue a life of sacrifice: a true sense of penance and mortification. One of the most dangerous consequences of modernism has been the profound shift specifically in the perception of Christian practices of mortification and penance.

Often when we read about traditional Christian practices of penance and mortification in the media, these forms of sacrifice are treated as archaic actions taken by saints of old as penance to avoid eternal punishment. We read about hair shirts and other mortifications and are told that they are superstitious traditions that some extremists believe will get them to Heaven. Salvation by works!

If you believe the lies of the culture, then you believe the act of giving up your morning latte or your glass of wine with

---

[93] *The 12 Steps to Holiness and Salvation,* 139.

dinner has zero spiritual benefit; it is merely a matter of cutting calories. But in fact, the spiritual benefits of choices carried out in the physical world can be profound when those sacrifices are offered in love. The Church has long taught that sacrifices in the physical realm can have an amazing effect on our souls and on the souls of those around us. Penance and mortification become sacrifices when they are offered as a means to demonstrate to God our adoration and gratitude, supplication and communion (see CCC 2099). In this way, choices that we make in the physical world can dramatically affect both the Body of Christ and our own efforts to grow in holiness.

Two of the most important passages in Sacred Scripture speak directly to penance and mortification, and we have all but dismissed them. Consider the first words of John the Baptist: "Repent, for the kingdom of heaven is at hand" (Matt. 3:2). And recall the first words of Jesus as He began His ministry: "Repent, for the kingdom of heaven is at hand" (Matt. 4:17). The *Catechism* explains that interior repentance is really about conversion: "Interior repentance is a radical reorientation of our whole life, a return, a conversion to God with all our heart, an end of sin" (1431). What is penance but the exterior expression of that interior repentance? (see CCC 1434). Additionally, the words that have driven this entire book are the words expressed by Jesus: "If any man would come after me, let him deny himself, take up his cross and follow me" (Matt. 16:24). The practice of mortification is simply the act of "denying oneself."

Penance is a supernatural undertaking. The Very Reverend Adolphe Tanquerey defines it as "a supernatural virtue, allied to justice, which inclines the sinner to detest his sin because it is an offense against God, and to form the firm resolve of avoiding sin in the future, and of atoning for it."[94] In other words, performing a penance helps you to hate sin and to resolve not to commit sin in the future, and it also serves as a kind of antidote that you release into the world to overcome the poison that you released through your sin. The Church lays out three forms of penance, which you've no doubt heard repeated over and over again during Lent (which itself is a time set aside for penance and abstinence): prayer, fasting, and almsgiving. Countless resources are available on each, so although I am mentioning them all under penance, they are each part of the law of the New Testament: the law of Love (see CCC 1969, 1972). As such, each serves a multitude of purposes in addition to penance (including mortification), and in the interest of space, I will speak only briefly and generally about each.

Mortification is the very act of denying oneself, taking up one's cross, and following Christ, as He mandates in Sacred Scripture (Luke 9:23–24). The word *mortify* comes from the Latin word *mors*, which means "death." To mortify oneself is to die to oneself. This is what the entire Gospel hinges upon, and it is a concept we must embrace if we wish to deepen our interior life because it is absolutely critical to a life of sacrifice.

Mortification plays a part in penance, but it is more directed toward safeguarding us from temptation. This is done by helping us to turn our senses away from pleasure, which is a key source of sin.

I'll be honest. I never heard the word *mortification* until I joined the Church, but even then, like many Catholics, I threw it out as something that only saints did—hair shirts and chains, extreme fasting and mutilation; that was only for those *really* holy people, and God didn't call me to that level of sacrifice.

---

[94] Tanquerey, *The Spiritual Life*, 341.

It wasn't until I read St. Thérèse of Lisieux's autobiography, *The Story of a Soul*, that I realized how small sacrifices were as valuable for my sanctification, if not more so, than those great sacrifices made by saints. I'll never forget my first "bodily mortification" for love of Jesus. I know this sounds ridiculous (I started small, let me assure you), but all my life, I had used two towels when I showered: one for my hair and one for my body. If we stayed in a hotel, I always had to ask for extra towels, because I wasn't about to make do with less. When we visited people and they gave me one towel, I always asked for an extra. I couldn't conceive of doing things differently.

Shortly after reading *Story of a Soul*, I remember telling myself, "I am never again going to use two towels." While this might not seem the most onerous of sacrifices, you have to start somewhere, right? Anyway, I did it that morning. It was strange. It felt like a big sacrifice. But in a weird way, it also felt good. I remember telling Jesus that I loved Him more than that extra towel, and I offered my discomfort to Him. I truly felt that I was giving Him a gift, no matter how small—and it was definitely a gift from the heart.

For the first few weeks, using one towel was a challenge, as, I suppose, breaking any old habit is. It was uncomfortable and a little awkward. Over time, this minor discipline I placed upon myself was no longer a sacrifice. Instead, it became a habit. This is how we grow in holiness. Little by little, we mortify ourselves of the world of the flesh, and eventually, we can achieve a level of detachment that is essential for the spiritual life.

There are several types of mortification. We are most familiar with mortification of the body, which includes fasting and other means of subduing the physical body for the good of the soul. For example, I knew of a lady who fasted from Friday afternoon until Sunday morning, to unite herself to Christ from the time He died on the Cross until he emerged from the tomb. Additionally, there is mortification of the mind, including the memory and the imagination, wherein we safeguard our minds against distractions and temptations that deter us from virtue. This might mean avoiding social media or abstaining from television and movies or anything that might distract us from pursuing virtue. Other examples might include intentionally training ourselves to control our thoughts or our tongue, which is an organ of the mind. Finally, we mortify ourselves to control our passions and direct them toward the good.[95] For example, we might give up eating at restaurants for a week and offer the money that we save to serve the poor. Or we might refrain from allowing ourselves to listen to music or watch videos with profanity, unnecessary nudity, or gratuitous violence. In their place, we might seek out inspirational music, videos, or movies that serve to encourage us in our pursuit of Heaven.

We live in a world full of self-indulgence, and we are all products of that world. "I want what I want when I want it and I deserve to have it, so don't tell me to restrain myself!" Isn't that the mantra? Sadly, I heard it said recently that the world has decided it doesn't need God, and people have been hanging on to worldly pleasures because they have to grasp onto something. Lord, have mercy on us.

PRAYER

St. Thérèse of Lisieux defined prayer as "a surge of the heart; a simple look turned toward heaven" (CCC 2558). You may think

---

[95] Tanquerey, *The Spiritual Life*, 378.

nothing happens when you pray, but, as Mother Teresa advised, dispose yourself to God's goodness and pray without ceasing. God is there. He may not always say yes if you make a request; but any prayer that seeks God as its end will always be answered in the affirmative. When I was in high school, I was not at all sure there was a God. I would have called myself an agnostic at best and teetering on the brink of atheism. I prayed at that time, "God, if You are real, I want to *know* You are real. I want to know beyond a shadow of a doubt that You are there." Well, it took years, but He answered that prayer in spades.

Prayer serves as penance as well. It is a way to express to God our contrition for sin and our desire to change and is also a way to make amends for the sins we've committed.

FASTING

Fasting can serve as a penance, a reparation for sin. But it can also serve as a form of prayer, as an expression of love for God, and a sacrifice for a particular intention. Fasting liberates us from our passions and serves as a medicine to heal us from intemperance.[96] In the Bible, Jesus provides instruction on how to fast: "When you fast, do not look dismal, like the hypocrites, for they disfigure their faces that their fasting may be seen by men. Truly, I say to you, they have their reward. But when you fast, anoint your head and wash your face, that your fasting may not be seen by men but by your Father who is in secret; and your Father who sees in secret will reward you" (Matt. 6:16–18).

---

[96] Paul VI, Apostolic Constitution *Paenitemini* (February 17, 1966), http://www.vatican.va/content/paul-vi/en/apost_constitutions/documents/hf_p-vi_apc_19660217_paenitemini.html.

I've seen the fruits of fasting. I have a good friend who married a non-Catholic. Rather than pull out the *Catechism* and try to prove to him that the Catholic Church was the one true Church, she spent her time in silence, praying and fasting. She never invited her husband to Mass with her. This may seem the opposite of what one who sought to evangelize would do, but she says she respected her husband's faith and his free will. Additionally, she also never left her children home with him when she went to Mass—even when they were babies; she made that choice because she didn't want her faith to be a burden to her husband. Three years after she began fasting for his conversion, her husband "suddenly" mentioned that he wanted to enter RCIA. The following Easter, he entered the Church, and today they celebrate the sacraments as a family.

Maybe you are curious as to what this friend's fasting regimen looked like. Well, I asked her because I wanted to know as well. She said that she fasted on Wednesdays and Fridays for three years before her husband's conversion. On those days, she ate some form of dry bread and coffee for breakfast and lunch, and refrained from snacking between meals. At dinner, she ate whatever she made for the family, only she strictly limited her portions. She did not refrain from dinner because she didn't want her husband to worry or become suspicious.

ALMSGIVING

According to *The Catholic Encyclopedia*, almsgiving is "any material favor done to assist the needy."[97] Almsgiving is an act of

---

[97] J. D. O'Neill, "Alms and Almsgiving," *The Catholic Encyclopedia* (New York: Robert Appleton Company, 1907), New Advent, http://www.newadvent.org/cathen/01328f.htm.

charity, done for the eyes of God alone, and is thus a way to combine love of God and love of neighbor. Alms can be offered as an act of penance (CCC 1434, 1438), as an act of piety (CCC 575, 2101), on behalf of the dead (CCC 1032), or simply as an act of worship of God in gratitude for the many gifts we've been given (CCC 1969). Almsgiving provides us with a tangible opportunity to show a special love for the poor, the underprivileged, the imprisoned, and the outcast. It allows us to emulate Christ by denying ourselves in order to have an immediate impact on the life of another.

13

Love of God: Giving God Your Time

You shall love the Lord your God with all your heart,
and with all your soul, and with all your mind.
This is the great and first commandment.

—Matthew 22:37–38

The goal of this book is to ignite in every Christian a desire to serve the Living Flame of Love, which knows no limits, recognizes no boundaries, and holds back nothing for Himself. So how can you strengthen your soul for love of God? I'm so glad you asked!

GIVE YOUR TIME TO GOD

There are two areas in which time is key in the spiritual life. Both require great sacrifice. The first is the time we intentionally set aside to spend with Our Lord, whether in silence, prayer, adoration, spiritual reading, or some combination thereof. The second is every single other moment.

Schedule Time Daily

Over the years, I've been blessed with some pretty amazing friends. Many of them have moved away, and I feel guilty about not trying harder to keep in touch. It's not that I don't have great intentions, but great intentions don't amount to much when there are more immediate demands on my time. These include yearbook committee meetings and speech competitions, choir practice and art class, not to mention five days per week of homeschooling with home management activities to be completed over the weekend (lest we collapse beneath a mountain of chaos come Monday morning).

With all the demands of life staring me down, the only way I'm going to visit old friends is if I purchase airfare and block off the calendar. *That's* when my intention will become a *commitment*.

And that's how it is with God. We may desire to visit with Him each day. But intentions don't matter much if we're unwilling to make a commitment.

Do you give God His due? Is He the first person you think about when you wake each morning and your last thought as you drift off to sleep at night? In my case, I may think of God as I drift off to sleep, but unless I'm very careful, I've been known to begin my day on a mission to complete a mile-long list, consisting of everything from the appointments that must be attended to my pipe-dream items, such as organizing the back corner of our basement storage area. Unfortunately, if this list doesn't begin with God, not only does my day inevitably end up less productive, but often God just doesn't make the list.

The *Catechism* tells us, "Following Christ and united with Him (cf. Jn 15:5), Christians strive to be 'imitators of God as beloved children, and walk in love' (Eph 5:1–2) by conforming their thoughts, words and actions to the 'mind ... which is yours in Christ Jesus' (Phil. 2:5), and *by following His example* (cf. Jn 13:12–16)" (1694, emphasis mine).

There is no way around it. Human beings will follow the example placed before them. If that example is not God, surely there will be another more than willing to take His place. Without any effort at all, we are bombarded daily with the values and priorities of this world. Negative cultural messages are constantly communicated via movies, television, songs, literature, advertising, and the like. If we don't make a commitment to spend time daily with Christ, won't we absorb the more *constant* influences in our lives?

- If you can offer God five minutes per day right now, then begin. Then increase the time you spend by adding five minutes per day until you reach a time that works well for you.

- Schedule time for spiritual reading. In case you are looking for some ideas, I have an entire book on that very subject. Check out *How to Read Your Way to Heaven* and begin a spiritual reading program.

- Schedule an annual retreat. Most of my more profound moments of introspection and union with Our Blessed Lord have come as direct results of retreats. Retreats allow you to rid yourself of the world absolutely for a time, increasing opportunities for interior recollection and spiritual growth.

RECOGNIZE THAT YOUR TIME IS NOT YOUR OWN

In his classic *The Screwtape Letters*, C. S. Lewis gives a profound commentary on time. From the mouth of Screwtape (a high-ranking devil), we are reminded in a not-so-subtle fashion that our time is really not our own:

Men are not angered by mere misfortune but by misfortune conceived as injury. And the sense of injury depends on the feeling that a legitimate claim has been denied. The more claims on life, therefore, that your patient can be induced to make, the more often he will feel injured and, as a result, ill-tempered. Now you will have noticed that nothing throws him into a passion so easily as to find a tract of time which he reckoned on having at his own disposal unexpectedly taken from him. It is the unexpected visitor (when he's looked forward to a quiet evening), or the friend's talkative wife (turning up when he looked forward to a tete-a-tete with the friend), that throws him out of gear. Now he is not yet so uncharitable or slothful that these small demands on his courtesy are in themselves too much for it. They anger him because he regards his time as his own and feels that it is being stolen. You must therefore zealously guard in his mind the curious assumption 'My time is my own.' Let him have the feeling that he starts each day as the lawful possessor of twenty-four hours. Let him feel as a grievous tax that portion of this property which he has to make over to his employers, and as a generous donation that further portion which he allows to religious duties. But what he must never be permitted to doubt is that the total from which these deductions have been made was, in some mysterious sense, his own personal birthright."[98]

Before reading this, the idea that my time was not *mine* never occurred to me. Each day, I would wake in the morning with a list of family appointments, household items, and community

<hr />

[98] C. S. Lewis, *The Screwtape Letters* (San Francisco: Harper San Francisco, 2000), 111–112.

service or professional goals, all composed by me, for me, and to serve me. Of course, I would have argued that my lists were created to serve my family or my community or even God. But if that were true, wouldn't I see His hand in the interruptions? Wouldn't I realize that He may have another plan for me today?

As a culture, we are all about controlling every waking hour. Just think about how we approach time. We prioritize it. We schedule it. We measure it. We race it. And let's be honest—sometimes we even "kill" it. Regardless, we know time is limited, and for the most part, we do everything we can to stretch it as far as possible before we run out. In the far recesses of our minds, we all hold fast to Benjamin Franklin's notion that "lost time is never found again."

I've created and recreated schedules running from morning till night, developed a rule of life for our family, and found efficiency in everything from a master housecleaning chart to a binder full of weekly shopping lists for complete breakfast, lunch, and dinner menus. I am a time-saving guru!

Until I get interrupted.

At that point, the game is over. It never fails. When something unexpected throws me off-track, one of two things is bound to happen. Either, like Superman's kryptonite, those interruptions render me weak, unmotivated, and unproductive (as in, "I didn't get X, Y, or Z done when I planned, so why worry about it now?"), or I get right back on track but am frustrated and short-tempered and no amount of "catching up" inspires an attitude change.

Does that sound familiar? Why is it so hard to go with the flow when life throws a curveball?

Consider this. Even if you've planned your entire day in a way that you believe will best glorify God, the fact is that *you* planned the day. But God may have other plans. Ask yourself,

"Is my true allegiance to God or to the 'masterpiece' I call my schedule?"

I'm reminded of a time when my daughter asked if she could "help" wash the table. Silly me. I believed her motivation was to help Mom. Since I had just washed the table, I offered her another opportunity. First, I encouraged her enthusiastically for wanting to help. Then I showed her a small pile of toys and asked if she wanted to put them in the toy box. She was deeply offended. She had wanted to help alright. But she wanted to do it *her* way or not help at all. Bottom line, she *really* wanted to play with a wet rag on the table.

What's *your* bottom line?

When God invites you to glorify Him by some means other than what you have planned, in your heart do you stomp off like a little child because you would rather do it *your* way?

There is a wonderful scene in the move *The Prizewinner of Defiance, Ohio* where the main character demonstrates this point beautifully. Evelyn Ryan, a wife and mother of ten whose husband is an alcoholic, rarely gets a chance to leave her home. She becomes long-distance friends with some women who invite her to join their club, called the Affadaisies, a group of women who—like Evelyn—win contests by writing short jingles for ad agencies. When Evelyn finally gets a chance to meet her friends in person, she and her sixteen-year-old daughter, Tuff, set off together on the long drive. On their way to the meeting, their car breaks down. While they wait in the August heat for the car to be repaired, mother and daughter sit on a bench, sharing a soda. Their conversation is priceless:

> TUFF. Do you ever wish you'd never married him?
> MOM. My gosh, Tuff.

TUFF. Do you?

MOM. No, I don't have any regrets.

TUFF. Come on, Mom. You've been stuck in a house for twenty years cooking and cleaning and taking care of crappy kids.

MOM. Don't use that word. Especially in regards to yourself.

TUFF. But you could be living in a city, writing for a newspaper, having an interesting life.

MOM. I do have an interesting life.

TUFF. Your life stinks. Gosh, Mom, just look at today. You finally get a chance to go somewhere and the lousy car breaks down. It's not fair. If I were you, I'd be angry all the time.

MOM. Well, that wouldn't do me any good, now, would it?

TUFF. For gosh sakes, you're only human.

MOM. Oh, sweetheart. Maybe I'm meant to make it to the Affadaisies, and maybe I'm not. But right now, I'm sitting here in the shade having a conversation with my wonderfully feisty daughter, and I intend to enjoy this moment to the fullest. And I suggest, for your own well-being, that you do the same.[99]

Perhaps one of the greatest sacrifices you can offer is to remember that, whatever the current moment holds, it is God's moment. And He has graced you with the opportunity to share it

[99] "Prize Winner of Defiance Ohio (6/9) Movie CLIP — Enjoy this Moment to the Fullest (2005)," YouTube video, 2:41, posted by Movieclips, https://www.youtube.com/watch?hl=en -GB&gl=NG&v=x9u_a8eEPlM.

with Him. Share it joyfully. Amid all your scheduling, remember that your time on earth is but a journey to your true home. You may reach home twenty years from now, or you may reach it today. What truly matters is not whether you used all your time productively throughout your journey, but how much love and gratitude you shared each moment along the way.

PRAY

In 1999, Gallup conducted a poll to find out which figures Americans most admired in the twentieth century. It may come as a shock to learn that the first person on the list was not a Hollywood A-lister (in fact, none of them were), or a big-business owner, or a politician, or a professional athlete (none of those either). The most admired person of the twentieth century was a would-be-obscure little nun who made her life among the poorest of the poor, offering hope in the face of hopelessness, bringing light to the darkest corners of the earth, and seeking no recognition or earthly glory for her efforts. The most admired person of the twentieth century was Mother Teresa, now known to all the world as St. Teresa of Calcutta.[100]

Day after day, Mother Teresa united herself to the suffering and the dying, rejecting the comforts of even moderation, choosing instead an austere and challenging life of physical hardship, possessing nothing more than a shiny bucket, her notable white sari with the blue stripes, and a devotional book. She and her

---

[100] Frank Newport, "Mother Teresa Voted by American People as Most Admired Person of the Century," Gallup, December 31, 1999, https://news.gallup.com/poll/3367/mother-teresa-voted-american-people-most-admired-person-century.aspx.

sisters did not plan. They did not build an infrastructure. Instead, they trusted completely in divine providence.[101]

What was the secret to her success? How was she able to live this life of extreme sacrifice that inspired people around the globe? In her own words,

> My secret is very simple: I pray. Through prayer I become one in love with Christ. I realize that praying to Him is loving Him.[102]

That union brought her to the fullness of life in a way few of us ever experience. In dying to herself, she found life, and she found it abundantly. Malcolm Muggeridge in his classic, *Something Beautiful for God*, says, "I never met anyone more memorable. Just meeting her for a fleeting moment makes an ineffaceable impression."[103]

Yes, but I try that, you say. Whenever I pray, I get nowhere. I feel as if no one is listening to me. My heart doesn't change. I don't change. I feel as though I must not know how to pray, and then I give up.

Mother Teresa has some advice for you:

> We want so much to pray properly and then we fail. We get discouraged and give up. If you want to pray better, you must pray more. God allows the failure but He does not

---

[101] David Van Biema, *Mother Teresa: The Life and Works of a Modern Saint* (New York: Time Books, 2012), 34.

[102] Mother Teresa, *No Greater Love: The Most Accessible and Inspirational Collection of Her Teachings Ever Published* (New York: MJF Books, 1997), 3.

[103] Malcolm Muggeridge, *Something Beautiful for God: Mother Teresa of Calcutta* (San Francisco: Harper and Row, 1971), 17.

want the discouragement. He wants us to be more child-like, more humble, more grateful in prayer, to remember we all belong to the mystical body of Christ, which is praying always.[104]

A saying that is attributed to Mother Teresa is this: "God has not called me to be successful. He has called me to be faithful." I always assumed this quote had something to do with our success in the political or social arena. But it speaks to our prayer lives as well. If only we stay the course, we can rest assured that God's grace will be abundant. So keep praying!

If you've been putting off praying because you want to do it "right," then stop now and offer your heart to God. If you already have a prayer life, but you are frustrated because you constantly get distracted or frustrated in prayer, then follow Mother Teresa's advice: keep praying. Don't let your setbacks derail you. Those setbacks, the frustrations, all the distractions — they are merely a means of helping you to grow in piety. Persevere!

RECEIVE HOLY COMMUNION FREQUENTLY

"Jesus took bread, and blessed, and broke it, and gave it to the disciples and said, 'Take, eat; this is my body.' And he took a cup, and when he had given thanks he gave it to them, saying, Drink of it, all of you; for this is my blood of the covenant, which is poured out for many for the forgiveness of sins'" (Matt. 26:26–28). Christ's words here signify His desire to provide us with the Bread of Life. In John 6 He confirms His intention when He says, "I am the living bread which came down from heaven;

---

[104] Mother Teresa, *No Greater Love*, 4.

if any one eats of this bread, he will live forever; and the bread which I shall give for the life of the world is my flesh" (John 6:51). He leaves no room for error, no cause for doubt. And yet, two thousand years later, just look at how we treat Almighty God at the altar of every Catholic church and in every tabernacle around the world? Do we recognize that God—actually *God*—is in our very midst? Or do we rush around getting ready at the last minute and stumble into church on Saturday evening or Sunday morning, slightly annoyed at having to *fit Mass in* among all our other activities?

The Holy Eucharist is the greatest gift that God has given us this side of eternal life. This gift is a sharing of Christ's life in us, a supernatural food for the journey through this life in preparation for the next—a sort of sneak peek into perfect union with God. For unlike all other sacraments, which are certainly good and accomplish beautiful work in the soul, in the Eucharist we receive not merely grace, but the *Giver of grace Himself*.[105]. The Eucharist is the source and summit of our Faith, the sacrament above all other sacraments. And yet how often do we treat it with ho-hum triviality?

This may be the greatest evil of modernism—to belittle and even ignore the great majesty and glory of Christ in our midst. Fr. Shannon Collins, in *Living the Eucharist*, points to attitudes indicative of our materialist society and the effects they've had on the sacred liturgy. He reflects:

> Modern man does not appreciate the Majesty of God nor recognize his own insignificance before the presence of

[105] Leo J. Trese, *The Faith Explained* (Scepter Publishers: New York, 2010), 347.

the Infinite, the Awesome. And at best, God is oftentimes seen as a buddy — a pal — and one can see this in most of the liturgies practiced in the Latin Rite. The Sanctuary, for example, in many parishes, has become more like a living room. The altar was lowered. Communion rails were a thing of the past — they defined the Holy of Holies and they might be perceived by modern man as being uninviting. Kneelers were removed from some places, for kneeling as a posture suggests that Someone is above us and that we're below Him. Church architecture, too, changed, for high ceilings and majestic interiors made modern man feel small, insignificant, finite. And instead of turning towards God in adoration, instead of facing the Lord of Lords, pleading for mercy, Masses are now turned towards the people. "Entertain me, Father, for I don't get much out of Mass." That became the cry of the modern participant in the liturgy.[106]

Clearly, Catholics must be educated on the absolute necessity of the Eucharist as spiritual food, without which our souls would starve. The profound significance of the Eucharist for our spiritual health is easily lost in its simplicity for a culture that eats not for nourishment but for entertainment.

And yet, if we are to engage in a life of sacrifice for the love of Christ, we must recognize with awe and reverence not only the great gift that Christ has laid before us and the reality of God with us but our absolute need to receive Him in Holy Communion.

---

[106] Fr. Shannon Collins, C.P.M., *Living the Eucharist* (Catholic Resource Center), DVD.

In *An Introduction to the Devout Life*, St. Francis de Sales shares some poignant advice:

> If men of the world ask why you communicate so often, tell them that it is in order that you may learn to love God, that you may be purified from your imperfections, delivered from your perplexities, comforted in your sorrows, strengthened in your weakness. Tell them that there are two classes of men who need frequent communion — those who are perfect, since surely they above all men should draw near to the Source and Fountain of all perfection, and the imperfect, in order that they may learn to be perfect; the strong that they may not lose strength, the weak that they may become strong; the sick in order to be healed; the healthy that they may not be sick; and that you who are imperfect, weak, and diseased need constant intercourse with your Perfection, your Strength, and your Physician. Tell them that those who are not encumbered with worldly business should take advantage of their leisure, and communicate frequently; and those who, on the contrary, are pressed and harassed require it the more, for he who labors long and hard needs solid and abundant food.[107]

If the torrents of grace available in the Eucharist were understood, grace would flow like a rushing river through great cities, rambling suburbs, and small rural towns, cleansing our hearts, purifying our souls and building each of us up in the Body of Christ!

If we desire to acquire a perfect love of Christ, receiving frequent Holy Communion may be the most important commitment

---

[107] St. Francis de Sales, *Introduction to the Devout Life*, 103.

we can make. For how could we carry this flame of love in our chests without igniting a passion of flames in our hearts? Frequent Communion will transform our hearts into a font of grace for others. Our desire to offer ourselves in love to God and for our neighbor will grow in proportion to the devotion we show to the Holy Eucharist.

VISIT THE BLESSED SACRAMENT

For many years, I received the sacraments, trusting that God had a reason for providing them, even though I felt nothing when I received them. I had an intellectual understanding of the Mass and the other sacraments, but that was where my appreciation ended.

Then I attended a weekend retreat where the Blessed Sacrament was exposed all night, and participants were invited to visit at their leisure. I should explain that during that time in my life, I was experiencing great distress and even anguish due to circumstances beyond my control. They were problems I could not reveal, even to close friends. They were very private and very painful.

Needless to say, I didn't rush to the chapel because I wasn't confident that I'd fare any differently than if I prayed in my room, where I was assured of privacy. The idea of spending time with Our Lord in the Blessed Sacrament did not excite me enough to make me risk running into other people by entering the chapel. But around 2:00 a.m., I was still awake and decided I may as well walk a short distance down the hall. What I recall of the chapel is a vast sense of coldness. There floor was of endless white marble tile with no carpet to muffle the sound. Every step, even in soft-soled shoes, seemed to reverberate off the great walls with an intimidating echo. But I made my way down the long center aisle toward the altar.

Kneeling in the first pew, I looked up at the Blessed Sacrament in the monstrance and began to cry. Boy, did I cry! What began as silent waterworks soon became open sobs, wherein I poured out my heart to Christ on the altar. Eventually, I moved from the pew into the center aisle and knelt at the foot of the steps, directly in front of the Blessed Sacrament. The cold I felt upon walking into the space was sharply juxtaposed to the tremendous warmth that emanated from the altar. I felt like a small child, sobbing to a loving Father who could take away all my fears and mollify every pain. I developed a peace of soul that I had not experienced in a long time. The profound nature of my experience that night cannot properly be described. But that's because words cannot express the triune relationship between Christ, His grace, and a soul in the state of raw exposure. It was palpable.

I am forever grateful that the amazing change that took place in my soul that night did not fade from my memory over time. Before that night, I had gone to adoration here and there. For a couple of years, I had a dedicated Holy Hour. But I had just been going through the motions. After this profound experience I realized that my heart had to be completely laid open and vulnerable for me finally to let Christ in.

I'll admit I am a hard nut to crack. The vessel of my soul is so full of the world that there is often no room for Our Lord. But He is *there*. He is *present* in the Blessed Sacrament. When not offering Himself to us at Mass, Our Lord, in His great majesty and power, sits patiently in tabernacles around the world, just waiting for us to come to Him. He is all love and all joy and all peace. And He appears to us in such a humble and benign way. His power lies in His love, not in His presentation.

Go to Him. Open your heart to Him. Spend time. It takes a good fifteen to twenty minutes to get rid of all the distractions of the world after running here there and yonder with cares and concerns and obligations. You need time to release all that before you will be able to open up to Him.

If you don't have a dedicated Holy Hour, I highly encourage you to get one. And if you do, consider adding another. Archbishop Fulton Sheen advised priests and nuns to dedicate themselves to a Holy Hour each and every day. He recommended that the laity do the same, to the extent that it was possible, and at the very least, that they stop in every day and pay Jesus a visit for at least fifteen minutes and still spend an hour whenever possible.

Whether once a month, every week, or even every day, if possible, that time with Our Lord is a priceless font of grace, illustrating that when we give to Our Lord, He gives back in exponential ways.

14

Love of God: Devotion to Christ and His Mother

*Then in spirit tenderly kiss the feet of the infant Jesus,
humbly extended on a bed of hay; and earnestly and
devoutly request him of our Blessed Lady, humbly intreating
her to vouchsafe to permit you to take him: receive him
into your arms, embrace him with tender affection,
attentively contemplate the sweetness of his sacred features
. . . placing all your confidence in his goodness.*

—St. Bonaventure[108]

Through the centuries, Catholics have been blessed with countless devotions, through which pious Christians throughout the world have been able to cultivate a greater love of and intimacy with our Lord. Devotions are special prayers and observations that are not mandatory and are not part our sacramental or liturgical prayers but have been passed down from generation to generation for our edification and sanctification. There are two very special devotions instituted by Christ and His Blessed Mother respectively, each calling us to make sacrifices for love

---

[108] *Life of Our Lord and Saviour*, 50.

of Jesus ands Mary, in reparation for those who have refused to love them. These devotions are particularly illustrative of the mystery of the Body of Christ, for their entire point is that our prayers, works, and sacrifices can make expiation for our brothers and sisters who have been derelict in their love.

PRACTICE DEVOTION TO THE
SACRED HEART OF JESUS

Between 1673 and 1675, Jesus appeared to Margaret Mary Alacoque, a pious nun of the Order of the Visitation of the Blessed Virgin Mary. He expressed to her His almost unbearable sadness at the blatant disregard and even rejection He had received from nonbelievers and believers alike, despite that fact that He had sacrificed so much for them. Here is Margaret Mary's recording of an apparition that took place in 1674:

> On one occasion ... Jesus Christ, my sweet Master, presented Himself to me, all resplendent with glory, His Five Wounds shining like so many suns. Flames issued from every part of His Sacred Humanity, especially from His Adorable Breast, which resembled an open furnace and disclosed to me His most loving and most amiable Heart, which was the living source of these flames. It was then that He made known to me the ineffable marvels of His pure love and showed me to what an excess He had loved men, from whom He received only ingratitude and contempt.
>
> *"I feel this more than all that I suffered during My Passion. If only they would make Me some return for My Love, I should think but little of all I have done for them and would*

wish, were it possible, to suffer still more. But the sole return they make for all My eagerness to do them good is to reject Me and treat Me with coldness. Do you at least console Me by supplying for their ingratitude, as far as you are able." (emphasis mine)[109]

Need you further justification for practicing this beautiful devotion that Our Lord Himself requested? Jesus desires nothing other than our love. Our gratitude. Let's see what this devotion involves.

According to Fr. John Croiset, the spiritual director of Saint Margaret Mary, "the devotion to the Sacred Heart of Jesus is a more warm-hearted and ardent devotion towards Jesus in the Blessed Sacrament, its principle motive being the extreme love which He shows us in this Sacrament, and the principal object, to make reparation for the contempt and outrages which He suffers in this same Sacrament."[110]

In His appearances to Saint Margaret Mary, Jesus had specific requests and also made rather generous promises to those who would love Him through this special devotion. For those of you that may be like me and question what the Church has to say about various apparitions and devotions, I can assure you that the Church celebrates the Sacred Heart with great fervor. Pope after pope has promoted its devotion. Pope Francis said, "The month of June is traditionally dedicated to the Sacred

---

[109] George Pollard, "The Revelation of the Sacred Heart of Jesus Paral-le-Monial, France," EWTN, https://www.ewtn.com /catholicism/library/the-revelation-of-the-sacred-heart-of-jesus -paral-le-monial-france-13719

[110] Fr. John Croiset, S.J., *The Devotion to the Sacred Heart* (Charlotte, NC: TAN Books, 1988), 56.

Heart of Jesus, the highest human expression of divine love. . . .
The Solemnity of the Sacred Heart of Jesus . . . sets the tone for
the whole month. Popular piety highly prizes symbols, and the
Heart of Jesus is the ultimate symbol of God's mercy—but it is
not an imaginary symbol, it is a real symbol, which represents
the center, the source from which salvation for all humanity
gushed forth."[111]

Devotion to the Sacred Heart includes the following:

1. Celebrate annually the feast of the Sacred Heart,
   which Our Lord Himself designated. Jesus' words to
   St. Margaret Mary on the occasion of this declaration
   make very clear what He would like to see on the day
   of this celebration, and also what the faithful can
   expect in return:

   > I demand that the First Friday after the octave
   > of Corpus Christi be set apart for a special feast
   > to honor My Heart; that, on this day, repara-
   > tion be made to It with special solemnity,
   > that the faithful receive Holy Communion
   > in reparation for the indignities which It has
   > received on the altars; and I promise that My
   > Heart will expand to pour out in abundance
   > the treasures of Divine Love on those who
   > render It this honor.[112]

2. Attend Mass and receive the Eucharist on the first
   Friday of each month for nine consecutive months

---

[111] Pope Francis, Angelus at St. Peter's Square (Sunday, June 9,
2013), http://www.vatican.va/content/francesco/en/angelus
/2013/documents/papa-francesco_angelus_20130609.html.

[112] Croiset, *The Devotion to the Sacred Heart*, 175.

in reparation for those who do not receive Our Lord, who do not love Him and who wound Him by their sinful lives.

Of course, this devotion is meant to be much deeper than checking these two items off a list. It is intended to be a devotion of the heart, a heart that swells with great love for Our Lord and that finds much satisfaction in demonstrating that love, particularly in regard to the Blessed Sacrament.

The following twelve promises are commonly associated with devotion to the Sacred Heart:[113]

Twelve Promises of Jesus to Those Devoted to His Sacred Heart

1. I will give them all the graces necessary for their state of life.
2. I will establish peace in their families.
3. I will console them in all their troubles.
4. They shall find in My Heart an assured refuge during life and especially at the hour of their death.
5. I will pour abundant blessings on all their undertakings.
6. Sinners shall find in My Heart the source of an infinite ocean of mercy.
7. Tepid souls shall become fervent.
8. Fervent souls shall speedily rise to great perfection.
9. I will bless the homes where an image of My Heart shall be exposed and honored.
10. I will give to priests the power of touching the most hardened hearts.

---

[113] A complete examination of the devotion and additional promises associated with it can be found in *The Devotion to the Sacred Heart* by Fr. John Croiset.

11. Those who propagate this devotion shall have their names written in My Heart, never to be effaced.

12. The all-powerful love of My Heart will grant to all those who shall receive Communion on the First Friday of nine consecutive months the grace of final repentance; they shall not die under my displeasure, nor without receiving their Sacraments; My heart shall be their assured refuge at that last hour.

You may be wondering why, if Jesus Himself requested this devotion and the Church has been celebrating it for centuries, you have hardly heard about it. I know I wondered. I still wonder. After I converted, I saw images of the Sacred Heart. Once I looked it up out of curiosity. But it seemed like something only extreme Catholics did. Or something that Catholics used to do but that wasn't important anymore. I was so wrong. This is exactly the kind of travesty I referred to in the chapter on the lies of modernism. Christ has not changed. He will never change. The world has changed. And to the extent that we are unfamiliar with the Sacred Heart, we need to turn over a new leaf. This is serious stuff! Our Lord greatly desires our love — not because it helps Him but because of the unlimited grace He wishes to give us through that love.

So if you already have a devotion to the Sacred Heart of Jesus, delve in more deeply! If you don't, look into it. You'll be so happy you did. God's love for us is unlimited. And abundant graces will be available to us if we practice this devotion.

DEVELOP A DEVOTION TO THE BLESSED VIRGIN

"To secure them from the hawk and vulture, she puts herself round about them, and accompanies them 'like an army in battle array'

(Cant. 6:3). Shall a man who has an army of a hundred thousand soldiers around him fear his enemies? A faithful servant of Mary, surrounded by her protection and her imperial power, has still less to fear."[114] In a world where the Catholic Church is constantly accused of launching a war on women, of thrusting horrible and even inconceivable virtues upon them — such as meekness and humility — that are intended to do nothing but oppress them, of not encouraging strength and power among women, but rather, hoarding all the "good" stuff for men, I find it remarkably ironic that the Queen of all women — our Blessed Mother — is at least as strong as "a hundred thousand men."

But wait a minute. Who exactly is this Mary whom we are called to imitate? Is she a meek and humble virgin? Or is she a powerful warrior?

Of course, she's both.

Contrary to conventional wisdom, Mary's power does not lie in her ability to pull herself up by her own bootstraps. Nor does it lie in her drive and determination. Counterintuitive as it may be, Mary's power lies in her perfect humility. One of the greatest paradoxes of our Faith is that in order to be powerful, we must first be weak. As St. Paul tells us, "But he said to me, 'My grace is sufficient for you, for my power is made perfect in weakness.' I will all the more gladly boast of my weaknesses, that the power of Christ may rest upon me" (2 Cor. 12:9). With her fiat, Mary, a lowly handmaid, lived this Scripture passage perfectly.

Responding to all the graces and treasures lavished upon her by her Father in Heaven, Mary handed herself over completely out of love for God, submitting herself to His holy will at all

---

[114] St. Louis de Montfort, *True Devotion to Mary* (Rockford, IL: TAN Books, 1985), 132

costs. In perfect piety, she gave herself completely and entirely to His plan. If only we would all do that — imagine how amazing this world would be! Unfortunately, the chances of each of us completely surrendering our wills to God are slim, as we are all handicapped by something from which Mary was protected from her very conception — Original Sin. We are trapped in what St. Louis de Montfort refers to as "earthen vessels."

Due to our corrupt nature, we are ever in need of devotion to the Blessed Virgin, for we do not possess that perfect humility with which she was so very blessed. In her exquisite humility, she stands as a beacon for those who desire to love God with their *whole heart, soul, strength, and mind* (see Luke 10:27). As we are incapable by ourselves, we must ask Mary to take us by the hand and guide us to perfect union with her Son. De Montfort explains:

> This devotion is a perfect way to reach our Lord and be united to him, for Mary is the most perfect and the most holy of all creatures, and Jesus, who came to us in a perfect manner, chose no other road for his great and wonderful journey. The Most High, the Incomprehensible One, the Inaccessible One, He who is, deigned to come down to us poor earthly creatures who are nothing at all. How was this done?
>
> The Most High God came down to us in a perfect way through the humble Virgin Mary, without losing anything of his divinity or holiness. It is likewise through Mary that we poor creatures must ascend to almighty God in a perfect manner without having anything to fear....
>
> We accomplish this by giving ourselves to her so perfectly and so completely as to remain nothing, as far

as self is concerned, and to be everything in her, without any fear of illusion.[115]

When you offer everything to Mary, she will take what you have and use it to mold you into the image of her Son. She will teach you to love Him with a perfect love, a love that casts out all self-interest and desires only Him. Through her intercession, God's supernatural grace will call us to say *yes* as she did. And who knows? You, too, may find yourself wielding awesome power in your lifetime: the power to convert loved ones who have strayed, the power to unite your family under God and to inspire complete strangers to come to know Christ through His Holy Church — awesome power ... born of your own meekness and humility.

If you — who are shackled by the concupiscence left behind from Original Sin — can desire good things and sacrifice for your children, imagine how much more perfect the desire and how infinitely passionate the intercession of Mary, your Immaculate Mother! More than the best earthly mother, she seeks only Heaven for you and will lead you directly to Her Son, provided you hold her hand.

Our Lady's Immaculate Heart

If there's any doubt about our call to sacrifice, one need look no further than the most famous apparition in all of history, which occurred in Fatima, Portugal, between 1916 and 1917. Just as Christ revealed to St. Margaret Mary His Sacred Heart, in the most famous apparition in all of history, Our Lady appeared to three young children in Fatima and presented her Immaculate Heart.

---

[115] De Montfort, *True Devotion to Mary*, 132–133.

The year before Our Lady appeared to the children, St. Michael the Archangel appeared as the Angel of Peace, and taught the children the importance of love and sacrifice, as though preparing them for devotion to Our Lady's Immaculate Heart. The first time he appeared, he directed the children to pray three times, "My God, I believe, I adore, I hope and I love You! I ask pardon of You for those who do not believe, do not adore, do not hope and do not love You."[116]

Lucia dos Santos (age nine when the apparitions began), recounts some of the second visit from St. Michael:

We were playing on the well. Suddenly, we saw the same Angel right beside us.

"What are you doing? Pray, pray very much! The Holy Hearts of Jesus and Mary have designs of mercy on you. Offer prayers and sacrifices constantly to the Most High."

"How are we to make sacrifices?" I asked.

"Make of everything you can a sacrifice, and offer it to God as an act of reparation for the sins by which He is offended, and in supplication for the conversion of sinners. You will thus draw down peace upon your country. I am its Angel Guardian, the Angel of Portugal. Above all, accept and bear with submission the suffering which the Lord will send you."[117]

---

[116] *Fatima in Lucia's Own Words: Sister Lucia's Memoirs*, ed. Fr. Louis Kondor, S.V.D., trans. Dominican Nuns of the Perpetual Rosary, 16th ed. (Fatima: Secretariado dos Pastorinhos, 2007), 78, https://www.piercedhearts.org/hearts_jesus_mary/apparitions/fatima/MemoriasI_en.pdf.

[117] Ibid.

The following year, on May 13, 2017, Our Lady appeared to the children for the first time. After promising to take the children to Heaven, she asked them,

> "Are you willing to offer yourselves to God to bear all the sufferings He wills to send you, as an act of reparation for the sins by which He is offended, and of supplication for the conversion of sinners?"
>
> "Yes, we are willing," was our reply.
>
> "Then, you are going to have much to suffer, but the grace of God will be your comfort."[118]

On her June 13 appearance, knowing that Lucia was suffering from many problems in her family, Our Lady said to Lucia, "Are you suffering a great deal? Don't lose heart. I will never forsake you. My Immaculate Heart will be your refuge and the way that will lead you to God."[119]

On July 13, Our Lady began by saying, "Sacrifice yourselves for sinners, and say many times to Jesus, especially whenever you make some sacrifice: O Jesus, it is for love of You, for the conversion of sinners, and in reparation for the sins committed against the Immaculate Heart of Mary."[120]

Little Jacinta, the youngest child to have seen the Blessed Mother, said to Lucia, shortly before she died:

> It will not be long now before I go to Heaven. You will remain here to make known that God wishes to establish in the world devotion to the Immaculate Heart of Mary. When you are to say this, don't go and hide. Tell

---

[118] Ibid., 82–83.
[119] Ibid., 84
[120] Ibid., 87–88.

everybody that God grants us graces through the Immaculate Heart of Mary; that people are to ask her for them; and that the Heart of Jesus wants the Immaculate Heart of Mary to be venerated at His side. Tell them also to pray to the Immaculate Heart of Mary for peace since God has entrusted it to her. If I could only put into the hearts of all, the fire that is burning within my own heart, and that makes me love the Hearts of Jesus and Mary so very much![121]

Additionally, the Blessed Mother showed the children a vision of Hell. Afterward, Lucia recounted:

We then looked up at Our Lady, who said to us so kindly and so sadly: "You have seen hell where the souls of poor sinners go. To save them, God wishes to establish in the world devotion to my Immaculate Heart. If what I say to you is done, many souls will be saved and there will be peace."[122]

In 1925, Mary appeared with the Child Jesus to Sister Lucia in her convent cell. She said,

Look, my daughter, at my Heart, surrounded with thorns with which ungrateful men pierce me every moment by their blasphemies and ingratitude. You at least try to console me and say that I promise to assist at the hour of death, with the graces necessary for salvation, all those who, on the first Saturday of five consecutive months, shall confess, receive Holy Communion, recite five

---

[121] Ibid., 132.
[122] Ibid., 123–124.

decades of the Rosary, and keep me company for fifteen minutes while meditating on the fifteen mysteries of the Rosary, with the intention of making reparation to me."[123]

Our Lady visited the children of Fatima on six occasions. In addition to her initial message, which was to "pray the rosary every day, in order to obtain peace for the world, and the end of the war," it seems her greatest message was that of sacrifice—that her children offer sacrifices of penance and reparation out of love and devotion for her Son. Additionally, she asked that we seek refuge in her Immaculate Heart, promising to lead to God all those who do.

How to Make Reparation to the Immaculate Heart of Mary

On the first Saturday of five consecutive months, with the intention of consoling and making reparation to the Immaculate Heart of Mary for our own sins, for the blasphemies and ingratitude of sinners, and for peace in the world, do the following:[124]

1. Go to Confession.
2. Receive Holy Communion in a state of grace.
3. Pray five decades of the Holy Rosary, including (at Mary's request) the following prayer between decades: "O my Jesus, forgive us our sins, save us from the fires of hell. Lead all souls to heaven, especially those most in need of Thy mercy."
4. Meditate for fifteen minutes on one or more mysteries of the Holy Rosary (this is separate from praying the Rosary).

---

[123] Ibid., 194.
[124] Ibid.

THE LOST ART OF SACRIFICE

For more information about the Immaculate Heart or the Fatima apparitions, the website AmericaNeedsFatima.org is a great resource, especially given the trying times we are living today.

15

Love of Neighbor

Come, O blessed of my Father, inherit the kingdom
prepared for you from the foundation of the world; for
I was hungry and you gave me food, I was thirsty and
you gave me drink, I was a stranger and you welcomed
me, I was naked and you clothed me, I was sick and you
visited me, I was in prison and you came to me.

—Matthew 25:34–36

A common attribute among the saints is an inherent under-standing of the intimate nature of the Body of Christ and their participation in that Body. St. Gianna Beretta Molla is a great example.

Most people think that Gianna is a saint because of the way she died. Since her canonization by Pope John Paul II in 2004, the story has been relayed many times. During her fourth preg-nancy, Gianna developed a tumor on her uterus. Although some advised her to terminate her pregnancy, Gianna would not allow her child to die in order to save herself. She chose to undergo surgery only to remove the tumor, but refused to terminate her pregnancy. Later, her baby was delivered via C-section, but Gi-anna died eight days later from complications. While her courage and heroism at the end of her life are laudable and inspiring, Gianna Beretta Molla offered her entire adult life—even part of her childhood—to serve others. As a wife, mother, and physician, she would certainly have understood the challenges we face in the modern world. And yet she took her responsibilities seriously and turned her response into great gifts for her husband, her children, and her community. If you read her biography, you will quickly learn that she recognized from an early age that life was not meant to be about *her*.

As a teen, Gianna began participating in Catholic Action. While pursuing her studies, in school, she decided to study medicine like her brothers. "Above all, she wanted to help her neighbor and give joy and serenity to those who suffered."[125] After World War II, when Italy was rebuilding its infrastructure and culture, Gianna became even more active in Catholic Action, taking on the role of president in the young women's branch. She was responsible for promoting spirituality and education among young women, serving those who suffered most as a result of the war. She was also active in the Christian Democratic Party in Italy, which sought to win the 1948 election after the fall of Fascism. Shortly thereafter, she obtained her medical degree and opened an office to serve mothers and children, obtaining a specialty in pediatrics. Following is a note from her journal about the responsibilities of a doctor:

We must care for our patients with kindness and gentleness, remembering that these are our brothers and sisters; have delicacy and respect. Do not forget to also administer to the soul of the sick person.[126]

[125] Blessed Gianna Beretta Molla, *Love Letters to My Husband* (Boston: Pauline Books and Media, 2002), 5
[126] Ibid., 8.

Gianna did not limit herself to serving her own community but studied Portuguese with a desire to serve with her brother Fr. Alberto, who, as a missionary, was helping to build a hospital in Grajaú, Brazil. Her brother Francesco was an engineer and was active in this effort as well. Gianna desired to help the mothers of Brazil who had little gynecological care during their pregnancies and through childbirth.

According to her biography, for various health reasons, her family discouraged Gianna from entering the missions, but "despite the disappointment of the moment, Gianna turned from her dream of becoming a missionary and focused her attention on her 'mission' at home."[127]

Shortly thereafter, Gianna met the man who would become her husband, Pietro, and poured all her love and devotion into building a loving family life together with him, placing Christ at the center of their home. In a letter to Pietro, she wrote, "I want to make you happy and be what you desire: kind, understanding, and ready for the sacrifices that life will require."[128]

In the ensuing years, Gianna did exactly that. Through their love, they were blessed with three children before what was to be the last chapter of her earthly life. Throughout her years as a wife and mother, Gianna chose to serve with great love and sacrifice from moment to moment until the very end. Here is an excerpt from a letter she wrote to her husband during his many travels for work (their son Pierluigi had to wear a brace because of a dislocated hip):

Our dear little angel is getting used to his brace; he puts up with it very well during the day (we try to distract him as

---

[127] Ibid.
[128] Ibid., 9.

much as possible), and he doesn't cry very much at night, even though he wakes up every few hours to turn over. He has a good appetite now, and a rosy little face, just like a little shepherd. And all this is because his dear Papa, who chose an enchanting little place with lots of sunshine from morning till night for us to have our vacation. I love to think that in fifteen days, you will be here with us to rest and enjoy this wonderful fresh air....

I found your second express letter when we got home. What a dear husband and saintly Papa our children have! Even though your work keeps you busy, you always find time to think of us and pray for your dear family! I can never thank the Lord enough for giving me a companion as dear, good and affectionate as my Pietro.[129]

Imagine if each of us approached marriage and family with such love and gratitude! Every letter between Gianna and her husband is filled to the brim with an attitude of service and self-sacrifice. Until the very end, when she was willing to give her life so that her fourth child might live, Gianna offered herself completely for her family as both a wife and mother.

You, too, have infinite opportunities to serve — whether at this very moment, when your child needs a listening ear, or tomorrow, when your church is seeking volunteers for a bake sale — like St. Gianna, you can offer yourself in service to God through the various roles you serve: as a spouse, a parent, a child, a friend, a neighbor, or a member of the community. Live each moment in grace, filling those you meet with the light of Christ.

---

[129] Ibid., 56–57.

I could fill an entire book with the idea of service. And I'm willing to bet that you could too. After all, Christ came to serve, and we are to emulate Him in every regard. He served through His humility, His compassion, His generosity, and His love. Essentially, He served through acts of selflessness, which culminated in the ultimate act of giving His life as a ransom for us. And He told us to do the same:

> Whoever would be great among you must be your servant, and whoever would be first among you must be your slave; even as the Son of man came not to be served but to serve, and to give his life as a ransom for many. (Matt. 20:26–28)

As Christians, we know that our calling is to serve. And for the most part, life offers abundant opportunities for us to live that calling. A perfect environment for growing in virtue and practicing this distinct calling to serve is the family. In His great goodness, God has given each of us a family that allows us to grow in the service of others. Pope John Paul II, whom Pope Francis called "the Pope of the Family," said this about the beauty of the family:

> The relationships between the members of the family community are inspired and guided by the law of "free giving". By respecting and fostering personal dignity in each and every one as the only basis for value, this free giving takes the form of heartfelt acceptance, encounter and dialogue, disinterested availability, generous service and deep solidarity.[130]

---

[130] Pope John Paul II, Apostolic Exhortation *Familiaris Consortio* (November 22, 1981), no. 43, http://www.vatican.va/content/john-paul-ii/en/apost_exhortations/documents/hf_jp-ii_exh_19811122_familiaris-consortio.html.

Service is a means of strengthening the family that has immediate and profound effects, both for our intimate relationships, and ultimately, for the world at large as we branch out to participate in society as a whole. The ways in which we can serve in our own families are innumerable. Of course, our families provide us with ample opportunity to serve — both physically and spiritually. Just think how we, as mothers and fathers, apply the spiritual and corporal works of mercy in our homes:

The Corporal Works of Mercy

Feed the hungry.
Give drink to the thirsty.
Clothe the naked.
Visit the sick.
Visit the imprisoned.
Shelter the homeless.
Bury the dead.

The Spiritual Works of Mercy

Instruct the ignorant.
Counsel the doubtful.
Admonish the sinner.
Comfort the sorrowful.
Forgive injuries.
Bear wrongs patiently.
Pray for the living and the dead.

Not only do we practice most of these acts of service daily in our families, but we are called to train our children to serve *lovingly* in each of these areas as well! (Notice the word *lovingly*: it's a sacrifice only when offered in love.) And for those of you without children, of course you have ample opportunity to serve your extended families, your communities, and so forth.

If you are willing to reach out and serve, the options are un-limited. The *love* that we show our neighbor is a direct by-product of our love for God. The two must work hand in hand, for it is in loving God that we are able to love our neighbor. Through His Word, he shows us the Way.

THE CORPORAL WORKS OF MERCY

Several years ago, I was responsible for organizing service projects for our local homeschool group. I opted to organize one event per month based on a corporal work of mercy. I called our local Catholic Charities and brainstormed with the outreach coordina-tor. We came up with several ideas, and we had a grace-filled year that provided an ongoing reminder of the intimate relationship between each of us and our neighbor. Below I'll provide some examples that we used as a group, although obviously the pos-sibilities for serving your neighbor are numerous.

Feed the Hungry

I made an appointment with Foodbank for the Heartland, and our homeschool group met there and divided large bins of or-anges into three-pound bags. There are often citywide food banks and several local pantries in most communities and they all treasure volunteers. Depending on the needs of the day, food banks might have you divide large bins of food, create emer-gency bags of food for families in immediate and short-term need, separate canned goods into boxes, or fill backpacks for kids who need food over the weekend or on other days when they are out of school.

Other ideas:

- Bring meals to new families or families that are struggling with difficulties.
- Plan ahead by collecting $10 gift cards to local fast-food restaurants and give them to those who stand on the corner with signs asking for help. For many years, I was severely conflicted about how to help those who begged on the street, especially having experienced — more than once — people who play the system. But advice from two women who work with the poor on a regular basis really helped me to love my neighbor without the baggage. First, they said, *do not give money.* This will keep addicts from using your kindness to inflict harm on themselves or others. Second, *encounter Christ in the person.* Roll down the window and make eye contact. Smile. Ask the person's name. Offer tangible help. Examples as an alternative to gift cards include giving a water bottle and a small prepackaged snack; have emergency bags readily available in your vehicle that may include a prayer card or a rosary, a granola bar, and socks or gloves if it's cold.
- Give food to a food pantry through your local parish. Volunteer to coordinate such efforts in your parish or community.
- In our area, every couple of months we receive a bag in the mail that is specifically used to collect food for veterans.

Give Drink to the Thirsty

Our homeschool group also volunteered at a Special Olympics fall football tournament, where we handed out water and hugs as players came off the field. What a special day that was!

- Sign up to hand out water at a local race. When our kids were young our family did this for the Kansas City Marathon, and the kids loved the excitement of that experience. I loved the example they had of hundreds and hundreds of disciplined runners who had trained day after day, month after month, to participate in the event.
- Make donations to organizations such as Cross Catholic Outreach, which brings clean water to those in need all over the world.

Clothe the Naked

Our group worked with an organization in Kansas City called Project Uplift, a nonprofit outreach for the homeless. We gathered at a local church on a cold winter day and loaded vehicles with all kinds of winter clothing, including coats, hats, scarves, and gloves. The kids had lots of fun loading the vehicles and enjoying a bit of hot chocolate and cookies afterward.

- Have a coat drive, or volunteer for one. Every fall in our area, the St. Vincent de Paul Society organizes a citywide coat drive, and there are tons of volunteer opportunities for it—from organizing coats, hats, and gloves by size to helping various customers select just the right coats for them!
- Donate your used clothes to nonprofit organizations that give clothing to the poor.
- Call your local shelter and ask whether they are in need of clothing. Provide some portion of their request.

Visit the Sick

Our group served the elderly community at Little Sisters of the Poor by inviting kids to do poetry recitations. After the "show," the kids shared a snack and made Valentines with the residents.

- Visit a hospital. Last year, my husband was in the hospital for several days. While I was visiting him, a woman came in and offered to pray the Rosary with us. We learned that she volunteers to visit the hospital every Tuesday night to sit, visit, and pray with people who often have no visitors.
- Set up a neighborhood, community, or parish program wherein families bring meals to other families who have recently had a baby or had a miscarriage.
- Do the same for families of those who are sick or who have gone through surgery or other medical procedures.

Visit the Imprisoned

We had lots of little children involved in our organization, so we didn't quite feel comfortable entering a prison environment. When a prisoner is released, one of the first things he needs is a job. We learned through Catholic Charities that, unfortunately, after prisoners have served terms of a year or more, many of their belongings have been lost, sold, or confiscated. Often upon release, ex-prisoners often have only the clothes on their backs. As a way to have an impact from a distance, we all brought essential personal-hygiene items—one family signed up for toothpaste, another for toothbrushes, another for razors, and so on—and then filled gallon Ziploc bags with the items and delivered them to Catholic Charities for its prison ministry.

- Get involved in prison ministries through your local Catholic Charities.

- Donate toward scholarships for children who have parents in prison.
- Collect Christmas gifts for families who have parents in prison.

Shelter the Homeless

Our local Catholic Charities made care packages for families that were displaced due to some major life event. They had a program where they would help families find low-cost shelter, and within that ministry, they collected donated household necessities and provided them to families as house-warming gifts. My homeschool group came together to provide basic household necessities such as toilet paper, paper towels, toothpaste, toothbrushes, shampoo, conditioner, soap, laundry detergent, and cleaning supplies.

- Volunteer for organizations such as Habitat for Humanity that build homes for those in need.
- Often parishes work with local homeless shelters — if yours does, ask how you can help out.

Bury the Dead

Our group prayed a Rosary and prayers for the Holy Souls in Purgatory at a local cemetery on All Souls' Day.

- Make it a routine to send cards to those who have lost loved ones. Have Masses offered for the dead, and send the Mass cards to their loved ones.
- Make it a habit to attend the funerals of people you may have known even marginally and join your prayers with those of other faithful for the souls of the deceased.
- Visit a cemetery and pray for the dead — for loved ones who have passed away and even for those you've never met.

THE SPIRITUAL WORKS OF MERCY

I have found that people are often much more familiar with the corporal works of mercy than with the spiritual works of mercy. Both are critical to our call as Christians. Below are a few "spiritual works" ideas to help you brainstorm. No doubt you've had plenty of opportunities to practice these even among the people closest to you!

Instruct the Ignorant

- Make sure you are learned in your Faith so that you will be equipped to answer those who ask questions. You'd be amazed at how a well-thought-out answer can inspire a further quest for truth.
- Teach! Teach RCIA or a children's catechism class. Bring passion and joy to the task and inspire a great love for God's truth in the Church.
- Offer to pay for someone to attend a spiritual retreat conference that you know to be based on solid Catholic teaching.
- Offer to take others to Mass, whether someone who needs a ride or someone you are encouraging to return to or initiate into the sacraments.

Counsel the Doubtful

- Offer a friend who is suffering a spiritual book that has been particularly fruitful for you.
- Help a friend in need to discern God's will for a decision.
- Help a loved one to discern what would be most moral and ethical path in a questionable situation.
- Live out your Faith as a witness, so that others may be inspired by the beauty of Catholicism and might

further recognize that Christ is the Way, the Truth
and the Life.

- Be attentive in a special way to a friend who is struggling. Take extra time to pray with or invite that person
to Mass. Offer to attend a Bible study, parish activity, or
retreat with him or her.

Admonish the Sinner

- When speaking with others about their sin, be gentle.
Guide others toward Christ without beating them over
the head. Remember that humility is key, and that love
covers a multitude of sins.
- After you address someone in great humility, walk with
that person down what may be a difficult path of change.
Do not abandon someone in need.

Comfort the Sorrowful

- Many years ago, I was part of a ministry run by our local
Catholic Charities called Grieving Hearts, in which volunteers sent personal letters to those who were grieving
the loss of loved ones. Check with your local Catholic
Charities for a similar program, or start your own through
your local parish.
- Be willing to listen to those who are suffering from loss or
tragedy. Our willingness to listen to those going through
tough times can make a huge difference to someone
who is suffering.
- Keep in mind that when people are suffering, most often
what they want is an open ear and not advice.
- Take a meal or send a card to someone who has suffered
a loss.

Forgive Injuries

- Never hold a grudge. Remember that in the Our Father, we say, "Forgive us our trespasses as we forgive those who trespass against us." Our sins will be forgiven as we forgive others.
- Apologize with a sincere heart when you have offended someone, and pray for God's mercy when you have been wronged.
- Go to Confession; the act of seeking reconciliation with God opens our hearts to reconciliation with others in our lives.

Bear Wrongs Patiently

- Quietly offer up your frustration to God, that He may do good with the wrong that has been done to you.
- Try to avoid being bitter when someone does something to offend you. Rather, give that person the benefit of the doubt, and pray for him or her, as well as for your own patience and understanding.

Pray for the Living and the Dead

- Attend funeral Masses to pray for the dead.
- Offer Mass intentions for others—both those who are suffering and those who have died.
- Keep a list of prayer intentions and offer them during your morning or evening prayers.

16

Perseverance and the Road to Holiness

Do you not know that in a race all the runners compete,
but only one receives the prize? So run that you may obtain
it. Every athlete exercises self-control in all things. They do
it to receive a perishable wreath, but we an imperishable.
Well, I do not run aimlessly, I do not box as one beating
the air; but I pommel my body and subdue it, lest after
preaching to others I myself should be disqualified.

—1 Corinthians 9:24–27

From moment to moment, day to day and year to year, we have
countless opportunities to unite ourselves to Christ through
our acts of loving sacrifice. We have discussed how to go about
cultivating a life of sacrifice through developing dispositions
that help us. In this regard, the lives of the saints can inspire
us. They stir up our deep desire for holiness and motivate us
to seek real change in our lives. But if you're anything like
me, no matter how much inspiration you find, things start to
fall apart when it comes to consistency. One minute we are
ready to offer everything, and the next we tell ourselves we've
worked hard enough and now we need a little break — some
pleasure, some "me" time. Pretty soon we find that our step

off the narrow path has led to weeks or months of indulgence that leaves little time or consideration for God. We all know this method will fail to serve us in the long run. And yet there we go again.

Let's consider the athlete who runs to *win*. There's such a grand difference between that athlete and, well, *me*. He has his eyes fixed on the finish line. He's not there to take in the scenery. He's completely focused on *the goal*. His mind and body are one. He is aware of the steadiness of his breathing, the muscles in his legs, the rhythm of his body and the ground beneath his feet, whether soft or firm. Throughout his training, he is careful about everything that enters his body. Nothing gains admittance unless it contributes to his overall fitness. Most importantly, he *loves* the sport. He is passionate in his pursuit, and his *desire to win* outweighs every obstacle. He's not sidetracked by other objectives; he has only one thing in mind: *to win*.

When it comes to sacrifice, perseverance is key. We don't sacrifice once and move on. Sacrifice must be a way of life. As St. John XXIII has been credited with saying, "The Christian life is sacrifice." And perseverance in that life is key to our salvation. The Letter to the Hebrews says, "Therefore, since we are surrounded by so great a cloud of witnesses, let us also lay aside every weight, and sin which clings so closely, and let us run with perseverance the race that is set before us, looking to Jesus the pioneer and perfecter of our faith, who for the joy that was set before him endured the cross, despising the shame, and is seated at the right hand of the throne of God" (12:1–2).

The letter sets forth Christ as a model of perseverance: "Consider him who endured from sinners such hostility against himself, so that you may not grow weary or fainthearted. In your struggle against sin you have not yet resisted to the point of shedding your blood" (12:3–4).

So *perseverance* does not just mean "muddling through." This is about *vigilance*. We are to endure to the point of shedding our blood. This is how serious we must be about fighting off sin. Sound like sacrifice? Absolutely. This echoes Christ's statement, "If your right hand causes you to sin, cut if off and throw it away; it is better that you lose one of your members than that your whole body go into hell" (Matt. 5:30).

We are to persevere against temptation, to withstand to the point of shedding blood, of severing our members. And yet how often do we treat sin as casually as if it were just a walk in the park, from which we can easily recover and catch our breath? How often do we fail to offer priceless gifts of love in favor of worthless moments of comfort?

Heaven is a goal, above all other goals, and we must pursue it with passion and purpose! Our eyes must be fixed on the finish line. We must release our attachment to the things around us. We must be completely focused on the goal. Our mind and body must become one in the pursuit. Because we are in training, we must be careful about everything that enters our soul through the senses—whether movies, commercials, pictures, stories, or conversations. Nothing may gain admittance unless it be edifying and contribute to our sanctification. Most importantly, we must love the pursuit. We must love our Beloved and desire to be with Him more than anything else.

Can we develop the passion and determination necessary to win? I am confident that through God's grace, we can. Just remember: "I can do all things through Christ, who strengthens me" (see Phil. 4:13).

CONSISTENCY IS KEY

St. Paul mentioned running. I know a little bit about running —I'm a jogger. Correction. I *used* to be a jogger. Now I'm someone who likes to slip my jogging experience into a conversation as though it has any bearing at all on my current lifestyle. Nevertheless, when I *used* to jog, I took my time. I looked around, enjoyed the scenery, never really pushing myself. Often I sped up or slowed down based on the speed of music rolling though my iPod at the time. I didn't quite have the fervor that St. Paul advocates above. My goal was always to finish—never to win.

It's not that I never set goals. But even when I set a goal and drove toward the finish line, my determination never lasted past a single race. I tend to get really motivated and work very hard—for a while. But consistent discipline is a challenge for me.

Let me give you an example. I've run two marathons. For each one, I was all in. I read articles. I researched training programs; I printed out day-by-day schedules that best fit my skill and ability; I trained. I rarely missed a run throughout my months of training. And both times, I was out of shape when I started, so I had a pretty long road to hoe. My husband and I ran our first marathon roughly seven months after my first son was born via C-section. Needless to say, I didn't even start training until six weeks after his birth. And even then, my first month of training could pretty much be categorized as *barely walking*. Fast-forward roughly three years. I ran my second marathon four months post C-section after my third child was born. I was determined. I trained hard—so hard that I shaved about twenty minutes off my first time.

But here's the thing. Between training years? Nothing. Not even a mile. When not training for a race, I was barely able to find the drive to run at all. You'd think I could at least run a couple of miles a day after training up to six miles daily and eighteen on the weekends. But no. Once I hung up my bib, I put my running shoes away for the long haul. Not intentionally. It just sort of happened. First, I wanted to rest for a day or two after the big race. And then the day or two became a week. And then a month. Pretty soon, two years had gone by, and I had barely run a sporadic mile, much less had a running schedule.

While training for the second marathon, my goal was to develop a lifelong program for my physical well-being, to build long-term habits, to be *vigilant*. But somehow it didn't turn out that way. I have all the excuses in the world: kids, house, commitments. No matter. The end result was the same. I trained. I ran. I quit.

I'm embarrassed to admit that I've given my diet the same commitment as my exercise. Maybe you can relate. One month I am committed to natural foods; the following month I dive back into the high fat, often highly processed comfort foods of my youth. Needless to say, at those times, there are plenty of chips, cookies, and even a little candy added to the mix for good measure.

In other words, I become slothful, gluttonous and weak.

Do you sometimes find yourself pursuing Heaven as I've pursued jogging and nutrition? Does your faith life suffer the same ups and downs? Have you found that when you are driven, all systems are go, and your prayer life, your sacramental life, and consequently, your spiritual life, are all aligned and fruitful; but then when you are not on a mission, not focused, you wind up feeling slothful, gluttonous, and weak? More lax in your behavior? Less able to withstand temptation?

It is true that in the spiritual life (as in the physical life), feelings wax and wane. We may go through times where we feel a bit ho-hum about the spiritual life. I know I do. There are periods where I am more casual about examining my conscience at the end of the day. I'm embarrassed to admit that my passion for Christ sometimes ebbs and flows depending on the spiritual book I'm reading at the moment. There are times when I find little excitement and even less drive.

I know that if I'm not careful, I'll create in my spiritual life the same sporadic, roller-coaster lifestyle that keeps me from making the progress I so desire in my physical life. Thus far in my spiritual life, I've been able to stay the course—for the most part. This may be due to the fact that I approach my spiritual health differently from my physical health. First, I *don't* think of every day between now and the end of my life. I don't think of my faith as a series of rules, full of deprivation and discipline to be endured for the *rest of my life*. I think more in terms of gifts to God that I can offer right now. I focus on today. There are a lot of things I can do for *one* day. And I can enjoy doing them. I do my best to keep a consistent prayer and reading schedule. I participate in the sacraments. I try to approach opportunities for sacrifice from moment to moment, as God presents them to me (because sacrifice is about surrender).

Over time, a consistency has emerged. Things that were once great sacrifices have become habits. I've moved past bath towels, and while I continue to mortify my flesh in various ways, I find myself focusing much more on interior sacrifices—patience, kindness, having a good attitude, releasing my time, and so forth. Little by little, I am persevering—today. And by God's grace, I will continue to persevere tomorrow. When the passion disappears for a time, I continue to offer what I can *moment by moment*. Before I know it, the passion is back. Thus far, it has been my experience that the very sacrifice of perseverance in the spiritual life bears the most succulent fruit of all.

While *I* certainly haven't mastered it, there are those who practice this kind of patient consistency in their physical lives. They may never run a marathon—they're not about big accomplishments and lots of hype. They seek no attention or accolades for their fervor; rather, they walk or run six days a week for twenty years or more. Or think of those people who do not seek out diet after diet, fluctuating between large amounts of weight loss and its alternative; instead, they maintain an overall disciplined approach to food that allows them to eat in moderation, to approach food for its nutritional value, and to be consistent in their habits.

The spiritual life works the same way. Persistence and consistency are essential. A sacrifice willed as a humble act of love is worth a thousand acts of sacrifice offered in fits of passion. Discipline, will, and consistency in pursuit of goodness over time are the keys to great holiness in the spiritual life. In fact, isn't virtue defined as "a habitual and firm disposition to do the good?" (CCC 1803).

I know people who are devoted to Our Lady. They pray the Rosary every day. Or maybe they pray a decade every day. They practice the Five First Saturdays devotion. They might attend daily Mass. Their particular devotions are not what is important. What is important is that, whatever their devotions, they are consistent. They don't waver.

Have you ever noticed that—whatever the area of life—those who are consistent tend to take their commitments one day at a time? They don't get intimidated by the idea of an endless string of obligations. No one can guarantee they will jog every day for the rest of their lives. But most people could jog today. Few can commit to a perfect diet over the next fifty years without panicking about missing their favorite foods. But most people could commit to one day of intuitive eating. Or to fasting for one meal. And many would be overwhelmed at the thought of praying the Rosary every day for the rest of their lives. But just about everyone can pray it today.

There's a reason Aesop came up with "The Tortoise and the Hare." Slow and steady truly does win the race. Our Faith is not about revving the engine. It's about climbing a ladder, step by step — or, better yet, as St. Thérèse puts it, "Your arms, My Jesus, are the elevator which will take me up to Heaven."[131] It's about making progress. Moving forward. If I run a marathon today and then sit for five years, it's very likely I'll end up in worse shape than when I started. If I am gung-ho about my spiritual life for six months and then stagnant for another six, is there any progress? Probably not. In fact, it's very possible that I will regress. But one gift of sacrifice offered today can lead to another gift offered tomorrow. And the next day. And the next. Like the tortoise, I can make progress bit by bit. Isn't that how athletes do it? Don't they pace themselves, maybe even holding back a just a little to ensure that they can finish the race?

So, too, with you. Only by pacing yourself can you truly win the race. And that is what you are called to do.

PERSEVERANCE AS A GRACE

Whatever happens, please remember that you are not alone. Our Lord did not leave us to our own devices on the path to Heaven. He provided us with many sources of grace to help us stay the course. Among the countless gifts of grace God provides for each of us is perseverance. The *Catholic Dictionary* defines *perseverance*

---

[131] St. Thérèse of Lisieux, *The Story of a Soul* (Rockford, IL: TAN Books, 1997), 141.

as "remaining in the state of grace until the end of life." This, of course, is impossible without God. That is why the Council of Trent in 1547 declared perseverance to be "a great gift" from God. How do we gain the grace of perseverance? Through regular prayer and participation in the sacraments.

The Council of Trent had some beautiful things to say about the gift of perseverance when it comes to living a life of sacrifice. In pondering them, you should gain much motivation and great hope that God's grace will sustain you on your journey:

> So also as regards the gift of perseverance, of which it is written, He that shall persevere to the end, he shall be saved—which gift cannot be derived from any other but Him, who is able to establish him who standeth that he stand perseveringly, and to restore him who falleth—let no one herein promise himself any thing as certain with an absolute certainty; though all ought to place and repose a most firm hope in God's help. For God, unless men be themselves wanting to His grace, as he has begun the good work, so will he perfect it, working (in them) to will and to accomplish. Nevertheless, let those who think themselves to stand, take heed lest they fall, and, with fear and trembling work out their salvation, in labours, in watchings, in almsdeeds, in prayers and oblations, in fastings and chastity: for, knowing that they are born again unto a hope of glory, but not as yet unto glory, they ought to fear for the combat which yet remains with the flesh, with the world, with the devil, wherein they cannot be victorious, unless they be with God's grace, obedient to the Apostle, who says; We are debtors, not to the flesh, to live according to the flesh; for if you live according to

the flesh, you shall die; but if by the spirit you mortify the deeds of the flesh, you shall live.[132]

Each and every one of us is called to be a saint. And perseverance is the grace given us by God that will enable us to offer each and every sacrifice, to climb the ladder of virtue, finally to reach our goal, which is Heaven. It is up to us to cooperate with that grace. Ask yourself, "What can I offer God today?" And then offer it. Each day is a new day. Set goals. Commit. And then persevere—one day at a time.

---

[132] Council of Trent, "On Justification," session 6, chap. 13, http://www.thecounciloftrent.com/ch6.htm.

Conclusion

Final Prayer for You

Make me love thy Cross.
—St. John XXIII[133]

At the beginning of this book, I stated that sacrifice is *hard*. Despite its challenges, my prayer is that through these pages you have developed a new appreciation for the inherent beauty of sacrifice, that you treasure its value both in this world and for the next, and that you've come to recognize in a special way the need for each and every one of us to embrace our role in the Body of Christ, to love God above all, and to love others as He has loved us. I pray that you are never satisfied with mediocrity but that, by God's grace, you desire to transcend to the highest level of perfection, ever ready and willing to die to yourself in order to rise with Christ.

May you be inspired by the supernatural value of authentic sacrifice grounded in love and be passionate about stepping out of your comfort zone moment by moment, day by day, to engage in sacrifice at a level that perhaps you haven't considered in

[133] Pope John XXIII, *Journal of a Soul*, 255 (quoting the Stabat Mater).

the past. (Or if you've considered it, perhaps you haven't followed through. Now is the time.) I pray that humility keeps you grounded securely in God's grace, longing to surrender to Him completely, and knowing that, in the end, your family, your loved ones, and all with whom you come into contact—and even those you don't—will benefit from your gifts of love. I pray that you recognize that every sacrifice—whether the cup of *coffee* you forgo tomorrow morning, your *time* given up in the afternoon, or the unbelievable *physical or emotional suffering* you offer up tomorrow evening—is priceless and serves God's Kingdom in an extraordinary way.

As you continue your journey through this *vale of tears*, may you draw strength from the ocean of mercy that Christ, in His great love for you, has made readily available for your edification; may you readily accept His invitation to participate in the salvation of the world, giving unique consideration to every action or inaction, thought or word, recognizing each for what it is—an opportunity to build up (rather than tear down) the Kingdom of God.

May you take this day, and every day, as an occasion to offer yourself as a living sacrifice to Our Lord (Rom. 12:1), knowing that in this way you will be securely united to Him, wrapped in His embrace for all eternity.

Appendix

The Discipline of Holy Mother Church

That proud reliance on self, or that cold formality, which may also be found in the Church . . . are not fruits of it, do not rise from connection with it, but are inconsistent with it. For to obey is to be meek, not proud; and to obey, for Christ's sake, is to be zealous, not cold.

—St. John Henry Newman[134]

In a conversation about sacrifice, we must discuss Holy Mother Church and her role as disciplinarian in the lives of the faithful. I am not speaking here about discipline as a punishment but about discipline based on the translation of the Latin word *discipulus*, which means "student."

The Church has no other role than to lead us to Heaven. As our Holy Mother, she prescribes certain practices for her children, like rules of the household. In the Catholic Church, the system of *rules* or laws and regulations that governs the Body of Christ in the practice of the Faith is called canon law.[135] This law is

---

[134] *Parochial and Plain Sermons* (San Francisco: Ignatius Press, 1997), 612.

[135] Auguste Boudinhon, "Canon Law," *The Catholic Encyclopedia*, vol. 9 (New York: Robert Appleton Company, 1910), http://www.newadvent.org/cathen/09056a.htm.

made or adopted by the ecclesiastical authority of the Church for the salvation of souls.

Pope Paul VI, in his apostolic constitution *Paenitemini*, described beautifully the Church's consideration of her interest in and responsibility in helping her children bind themselves to Christ and strengthening them against the temptations of the world:

> The Church, in an effort to arrive at a more profound meditation on the mystery of itself, examined its own nature in all its dimensions and scrutinized its human and divine, visible and invisible, temporal and eternal elements. By first of all examining more thoroughly the link which binds it to Christ and His salvific action, it has underlined more clearly how all its members are called upon to participate in the work of Christ and therefore to participate also in His expiation.
>
> In addition, it has gained a clearer awareness that, while it is by divine vocation holy and without blemish, it is defective in its members and in continuous need of conversion and renewal, a renewal which must be implemented not only interiorly and individually but also externally and socially.
>
> Lastly, the Church has considered more attentively its role in the earthly city, ... its mission of showing man the right way to use earthly goods and to collaborate in the "consecration of the world." But at the same time it has considered more attentively its task of prompting its sons to that salutary abstinence which will forearm them against the danger of allowing themselves to be delayed by the things of this world in their pilgrimage toward their home in heaven.

Through the guidance of the Holy Spirit, the Church deems certain practices most fruitful for our spiritual growth, and, like a mother who requires that her children eat their vegetables to ensure their physical health, the Church requires certain practices that are meant to nurture our spiritual health.

These practices are listed in the precepts of the Church as well as in the rules regarding mandatory fasting and abstinence throughout the liturgical calendar.

According to the *Catechism*, the precepts of the Church are "meant to guarantee to the faithful the very necessary minimum in the spirit of prayer and moral effort, in the growth in love of God and neighbor" (2041). This means that these are the absolute minimum efforts required of Catholics with regard to their participation in the liturgical (worship) life of the Church. The precepts are as follows:

1. Attend Mass on Sundays and holy days of obligation.
2. Confess your sins at least once a year.
3. Receive Holy Communion at least once a year during the Easter season.
4. Observe days of fast and abstinence established by the Church.
5. Provide for the needs of the Church.

FASTING AND ABSTINENCE IN THE CHURCH

The fourth precept of the Church calls Catholics to observe days of fast and abstinence as prescribed by the Church. There are two days in the liturgical calendar that call for fasting and abstinence: Ash Wednesday and Good Friday.[136] Most practicing

---

[136] *Code of Canon Law*, canon 1251.

Catholics observe these days during Lent. One thing to keep in mind as we discuss sacrifice is that these observances are not meant to be top-down rules imposed by a disconnected body for a strict enforcement of discipline. Rather, they are meant to serve as reminders of our union with Christ in His great suffering and death. In solidarity with other Christians, the entire Body of Christ observes these days. On Ash Wednesday, we publicly recognize that we are embarking on a season of penance, in preparation for Easter. On Good Friday, we mourn the death of Our Lord, and we fast and abstain in loving recognition of His sacrifice.

COMMUNION FAST

There is another fast that is observed in the Church. As Catholics, we are called to fast from food and drink (except medicine and water) for one hour before receiving Holy Communion.[137] This fast is meant to prepare our minds and bodies for the reception of Our Lord. It serves to create a "hunger" for Our Lord as we enter into the Holy Sacrifice of the Mass. This hour is considered a minimum; we may fast longer. Some people do not eat at all before attending Mass on a given day.

MEATLESS FRIDAYS

There is another discipline that remains in canon law, although it has been all but overlooked by most who are given the privilege of passing on the Faith to future generations. Before the rule on

[137] Ibid., canon 919.

abstinence and fasting on Ash Wednesday and Good Friday, there is another note in canon 1251:

> Abstinence from meat, or from some other food as determined by the Episcopal Conference, is to be observed on all Fridays, unless a solemnity should fall on a Friday.[138]

Did you catch that? We are called to abstain from meat, not merely on Fridays during Lent, but on *all* Fridays — that is, unless we've come up with some alternative sacrifice of food deemed satisfactory by the Episcopal Conference. We are called to offer a sacrifice every Friday in remembrance of Our Lord's death, just as every Sunday, we celebrate His Resurrection.

In 1966, the National Conference of Catholic Bishops released a *Pastoral Statement on Penance and Abstinence*. In it, among other things, the bishops reiterated the importance of penitential observance on every Friday throughout the liturgical year, not merely during Lent. Having said that, they acknowledged that, while Catholics have universally observed "meatless Fridays" as a penance, for some this practice no longer constituted penance. For example, abstaining from meat would not serve as much of a sacrifice for vegetarians. The bishops explained that we must each discipline ourselves in the spirit of penance, recognizing that every Friday serves as a mini Good Friday, wherein we prepare ourselves for "Easter" Sunday, as every Sunday is observed as a mini Easter. Below is a long quotation from the document that beautifully explains once and for all that we must observe some penance on Fridays; for most, the penance of abstaining from meat is still the preferable choice.

---

[138] Ibid., canon 1251.

Please note as you read, the bishops *did not* say that we need not abstain. What many Catholics heard—based on the number who dispensed with Friday penance altogether after this document was released—was that they were no longer bound to abstain under pain of sin. With that, 90 percent jumped ship altogether. Sadly, most of us missed the entire point!

The Catholic bishops of the United States, far from downgrading the traditional penitential observance of Friday, and motivated precisely by the desire to give the spirit of penance greater vitality, especially on Fridays, the day that Jesus died, urge our Catholic people henceforth to be guided by the following norms.

Friday itself remains a special day of penitential observance throughout the year, a time when those who seek perfection will be mindful of their personal sins and the sins of mankind which they are called upon to help expiate in union with Christ Crucified.

Friday should be in each week something of what Lent is in the entire year. For this reason we urge all to prepare for that weekly Easter that comes with each Sunday by freely making of every Friday a day of self-denial and mortification in prayerful remembrance of the passion of Jesus Christ.

Among the works of voluntary self-denial and personal penance which we especially commend to our people for the future observance of Friday, even though we hereby terminate the traditional law of abstinence binding under pain of sin, as the sole prescribed means of observing Friday, we give first place to abstinence from flesh meat. We do so in the hope that the Catholic community will ordinarily continue to abstain from meat by free choice as formerly we did in obedience to Church law. Our expectation is based on the following considerations:

We shall thus freely and out of love for Christ Crucified show our solidarity with the generations of believers to whom this practice frequently became, especially in times of persecution and of great poverty, no mean evidence of fidelity to Christ and His Church.

We shall thus also remind ourselves that as Christians, although immersed in the world and sharing its life, we must preserve a saving and necessary difference from the spirit of the world. Our deliberate, personal abstinence from meat, more especially because no longer required by law, will be an outward sign of inward spiritual values that we cherish.[139]

We must approach our faith, not as a set of minimum requirements that allow us to get by, nit-picking on the exact nature of this or that discipline. Instead, we must approach it as a relationship to Christ that is rooted in our union with Him, particularly to His suffering and death on the Cross. When the Church sets guidelines or rules regarding the practice of our Faith, she is merely a parent guiding us on our path to Heaven, helping us to avoid being distracted by the baubles and bling of the wide gate—the gate that advertises the easy way that leads to destruction (Matt. 7:13). Through various disciplines, she gently reminds us that we must continue to move toward the

---

[139] United States Conference of Catholic Bishops, *Pastoral Statement on Penance and Abstinence* (November 18, 1966), nos. 21–24, http://www.usccb.org/prayer-and-worship/liturgical-year/lent/us-bishops-pastoral-statement-on-penance-and-abstinence.cfm.

narrow gate, though the way is hard. For this is the way that leads to eternal life (Matt. 7:14).[140]

DOCTRINE VERSUS DISCIPLINE

Sometimes I hear people complain that the disciplines of the Church change through the years or by diocese and so forth and therefore cannot claim to have any real purpose.

The bishop of every diocese is the shepherd of his flock. It is his responsibility to work in coordination with the pope and his brother bishops, under the auspices of canon law, to guide us to Heaven, serving his diocese via the means he deems most appropriate for their needs. The pope along with all the bishops provide some amount of flexibility on practices that are considered disciplines and not doctrines. Mass on Sunday is mandated for all Catholics around the world; this has been passed down from the apostles, who were taught by Christ Himself.

On the other hand, while we all observe Ascension Thursday, for example, some dioceses have moved the feast to the following Sunday. This has been done for various reasons, including the availability of priests to serve all the parishes in their diocese on Thursday, or because Mass attendance had been markedly low when the feast is celebrated on Thursday. These are just two examples. Catholic disciplines vary by diocese for many reasons. But it is important to keep in mind that whatever the practices of your diocese, the Holy Spirit is working through each and every discipline as defined by your bishop, to best protect you from sin and safeguard your salvation.

[140] Tanquerey, *The Spiritual Life*, 205

About the Author

A passionate convert to the Faith, Vicki Burbach loves to delve deep into the beauty and truth found in Catholic spiritual traditions. Years ago, she began to notice a stark contrast between what she was reading and what she was witnessing all around her. In a world in which virtually every convenience can be found at the tips of our fingers, how could joy be scarcer than ever? To understand this paradox, Vicki had a great desire to immerse herself in these words of Christ: "Unless a grain of wheat falls into the earth and dies, it remains alone; but if it dies, it bears much fruit" (John 12:24). Her study led her to a new appreciation for the art of sacrifice—the narrow path trodden by saint after saint toward holiness, happiness, and eternal reward. This book is Vicki's attempt to share what she learned, not from the perspective of a theologian, but from that of a wife and mother, struggling daily with a temptation toward self-gratification.

Vicki has blogged about sacrifice and spiritual reading for the past eight years. She is the author of *How to Read Your Way to Heaven: A Spiritual Reading Program for the Worst of Sinners, the Greatest of Saints, and Everyone in Between* (Sophia Institute Press, 2017).

Vicki lives in the Midwest with her husband and six children. Her work has been featured and shared in the *National Catholic Register* and on *Catholic Exchange*, Big Pulpit, and the Catholic Education Resource Center, and she has contributed to study and leaders' guides for the Augustine Institute. Additionally, she has been a guest on *EWTN Live*, *EWTN Bookmark*, *The Busted Halo Show*, *The Son Rise Morning Show*, EWTN's *Morning Glory*, and *On Call with Wendy Wiese*, among others. She was the creator and moderator of a spiritual-reading book club at SpiritualDirection.com, which she led for six years. Today you can find Vicki's commentary at PelicansBreast.com.

Sophia Institute

Sophia Institute is a nonprofit institution that seeks to nurture the spiritual, moral, and cultural life of souls and to spread the Gospel of Christ in conformity with the authentic teachings of the Roman Catholic Church.

Sophia Institute Press fulfills this mission by offering translations, reprints, and new publications that afford readers a rich source of the enduring wisdom of mankind.

Sophia Institute also operates the popular online resource CatholicExchange.com. *Catholic Exchange* provides world news from a Catholic perspective as well as daily devotionals and articles that will help readers to grow in holiness and live a life consistent with the teachings of the Church.

In 2013, Sophia Institute launched Sophia Institute for Teachers to renew and rebuild Catholic culture through service to Catholic education. With the goal of nurturing the spiritual, moral, and cultural life of souls, and an abiding respect for the role and work of teachers, we strive to provide materials and programs that are at once enlightening to the mind and ennobling to the heart; faithful and complete, as well as useful and practical.

Sophia Institute gratefully recognizes the Solidarity Association for preserving and encouraging the growth of our apostolate over the course of many years. Without their generous and timely support, this book would not be in your hands.

www.SophiaInstitute.com
www.CatholicExchange.com
www.SophiaInstituteforTeachers.org

Sophia Institute Press® is a registered trademark of Sophia Institute.
Sophia Institute is a tax-exempt institution as defined by the
Internal Revenue Code, Section 501(c)(3). Tax ID 22-2548708.